MGLunn
2010

VALLEY FORGE: Traditional Land, Contemporary Vision

Dedicated to my wife Elyse, my daughter Mara and my son Matthew, who have encouraged and supported me in this endeavor and all that I do. Without them these images would not exist.

email: info@MJTiccinoImages.com

Thank you to the Valley Forge Muster Roll (ValleyForgeMusterRoll.org) for providing some of the information contained herein, as well as administration, rangers, interpreters, staff, and volunteers of Valley Forge National Historical Park (nps.gov/vafo), Friends of Valley Forge (FriendsofValleyForge.org) and The Encampment Store (EncampmentStore.org) who have been and continue to be supportive and cooperative in bringing these images to the public.

Printed with soy-based ink by Regal Press, HK

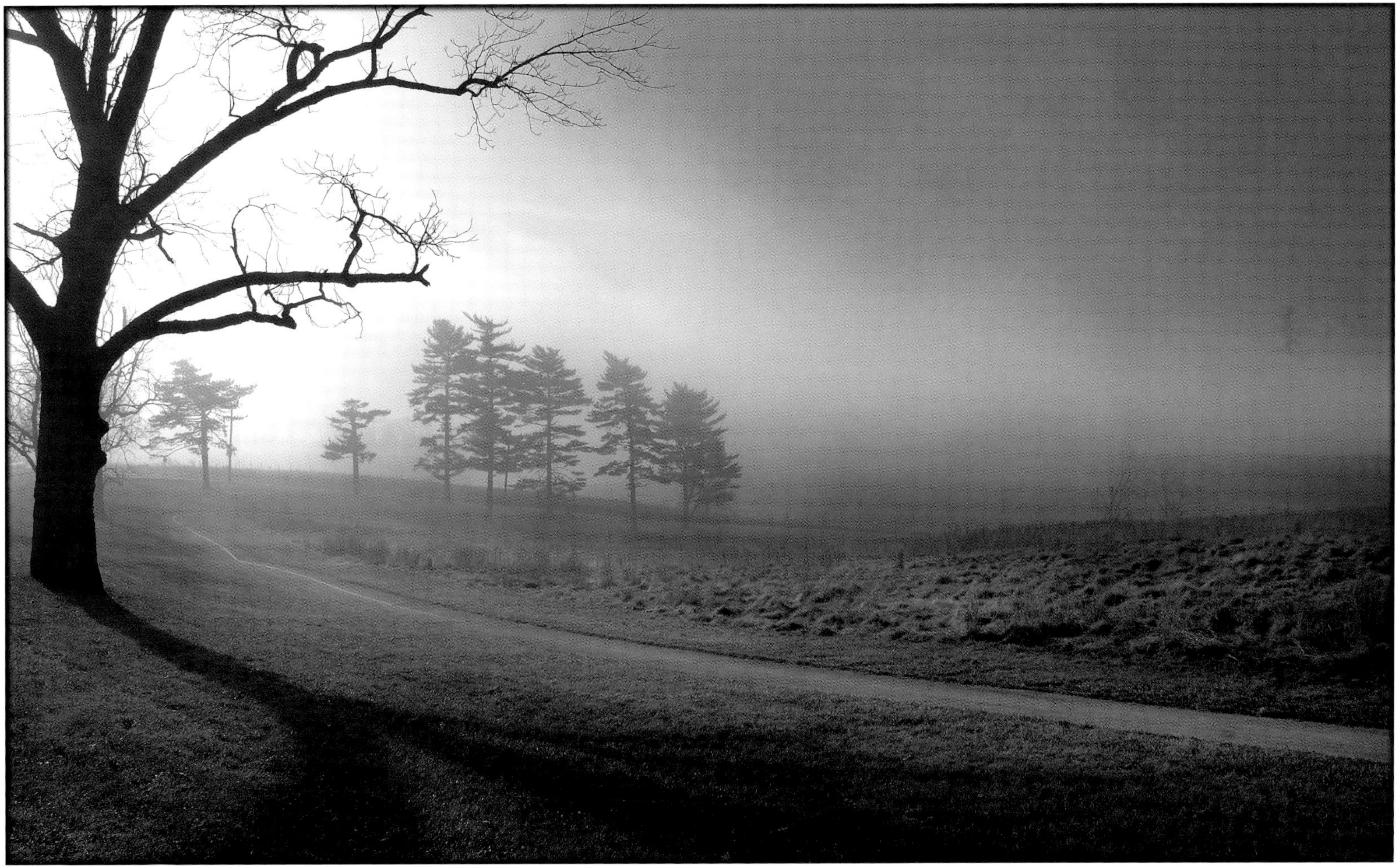

One of my first impressions of Valley Forge.
Early on a fog laden morning I fell in love with its landscape and its history.
This scene is where Rt.252 enters the park.

HISTORY LESSON #1:
THOMAS CONWAY

Born in Ireland and raised in France, Conway entered the French Army as a Lieutenant in 1747. In 1776, then a Major, he received permission to go to America. He arrived in 1777 and was appointed Brigadier General on May 13th at Washington's suggestion. He served in Sullivan's Division at Brandywine and Germantown. During the winter of 1777-1778, Conway was involved in an attempt to replace Washington as Commander-in-Chief of the American Army with General Horatio Gates. On December 13, 1777, Conway was promoted to Major General, but his embroilment in the so-called "Conway Cabal" convinced Congress to keep him from an active command.

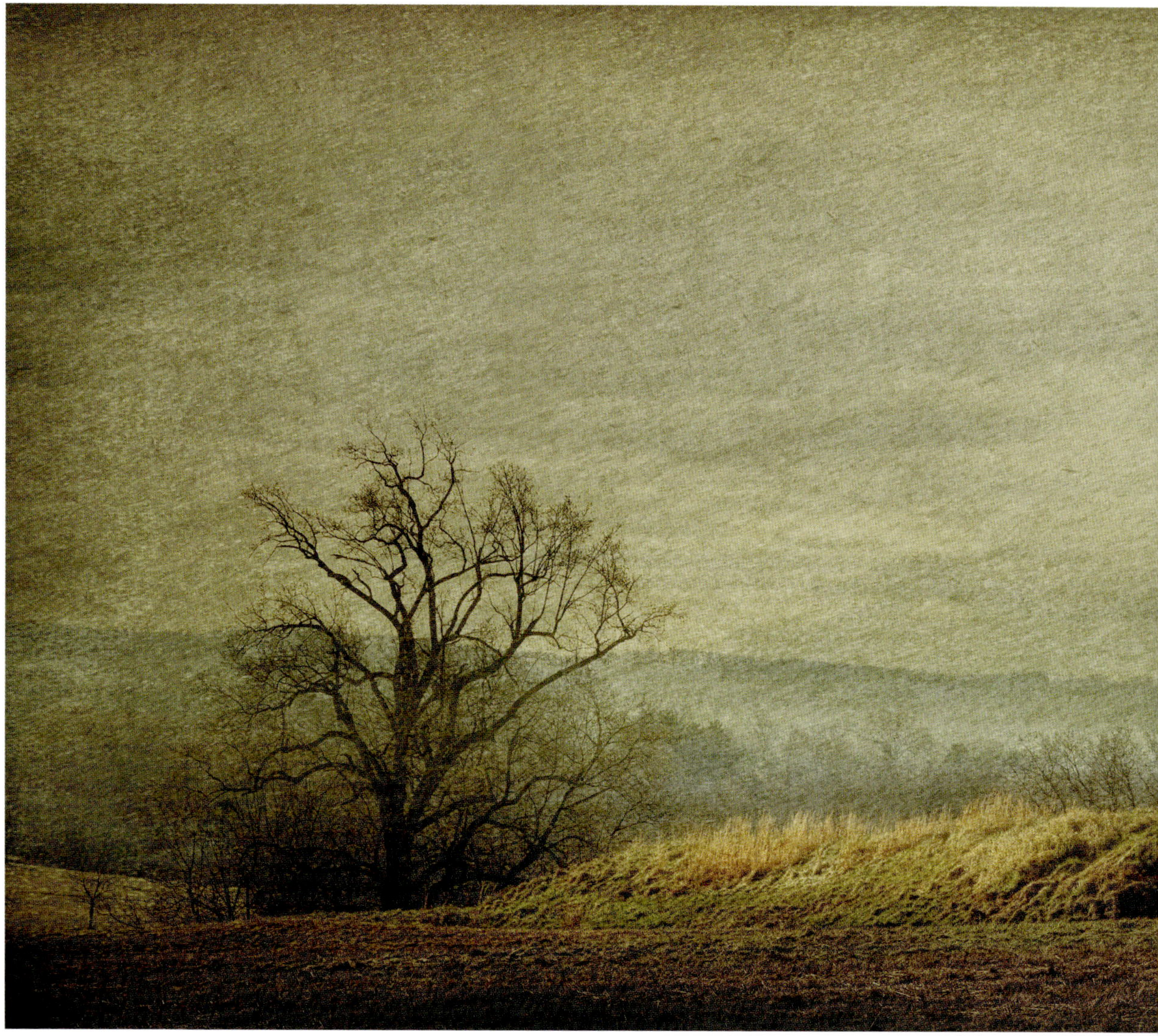

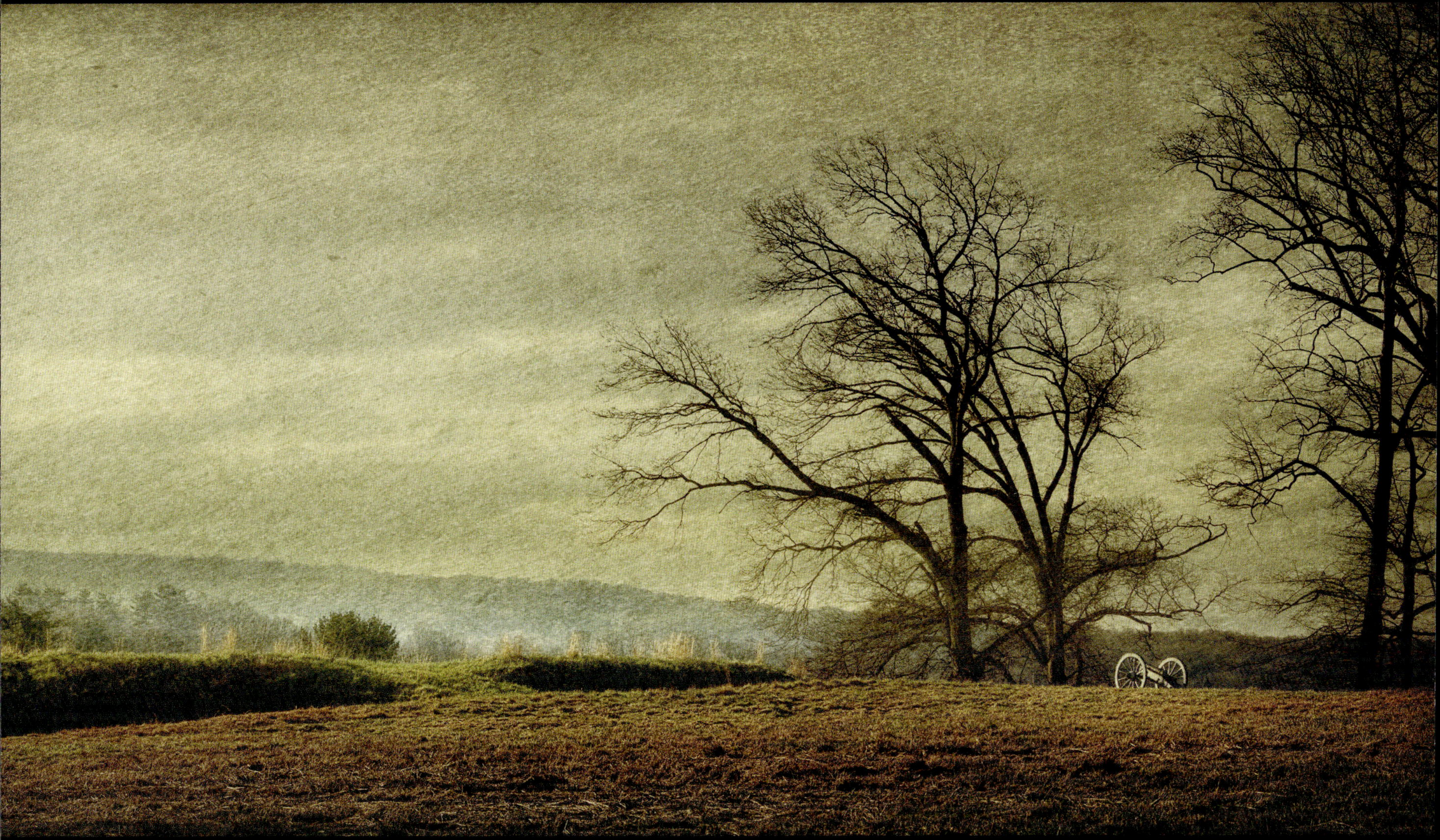

This is the view that overlooks Conway's Brigade. I have enjoyed many walks up this hill.

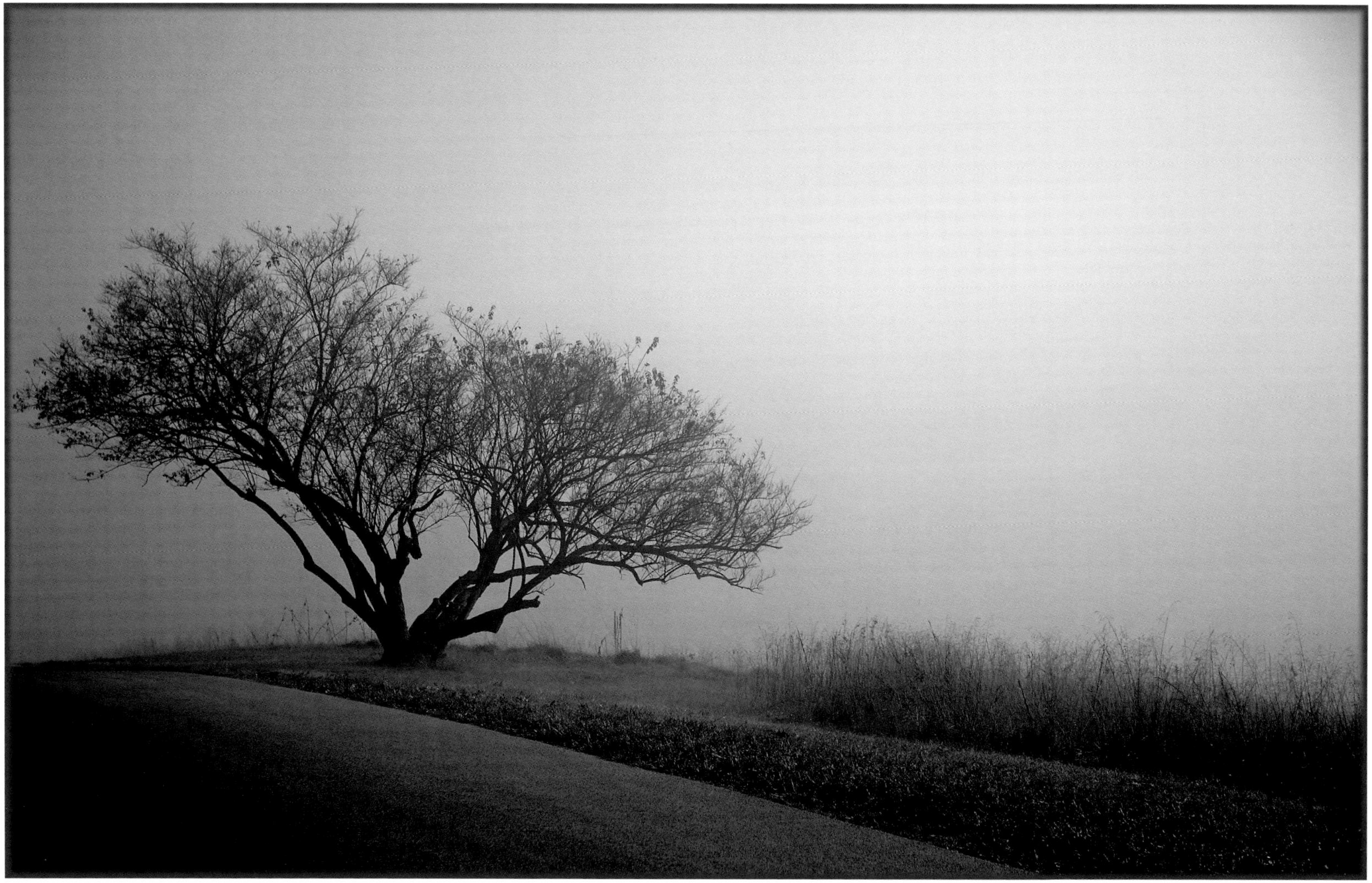

The park, as you can imagine is home to many trees; this is one of my favorites.
I call it "Split Tree" for obvious reasons. You can find it near the monument of Anthony Wayne on horseback.

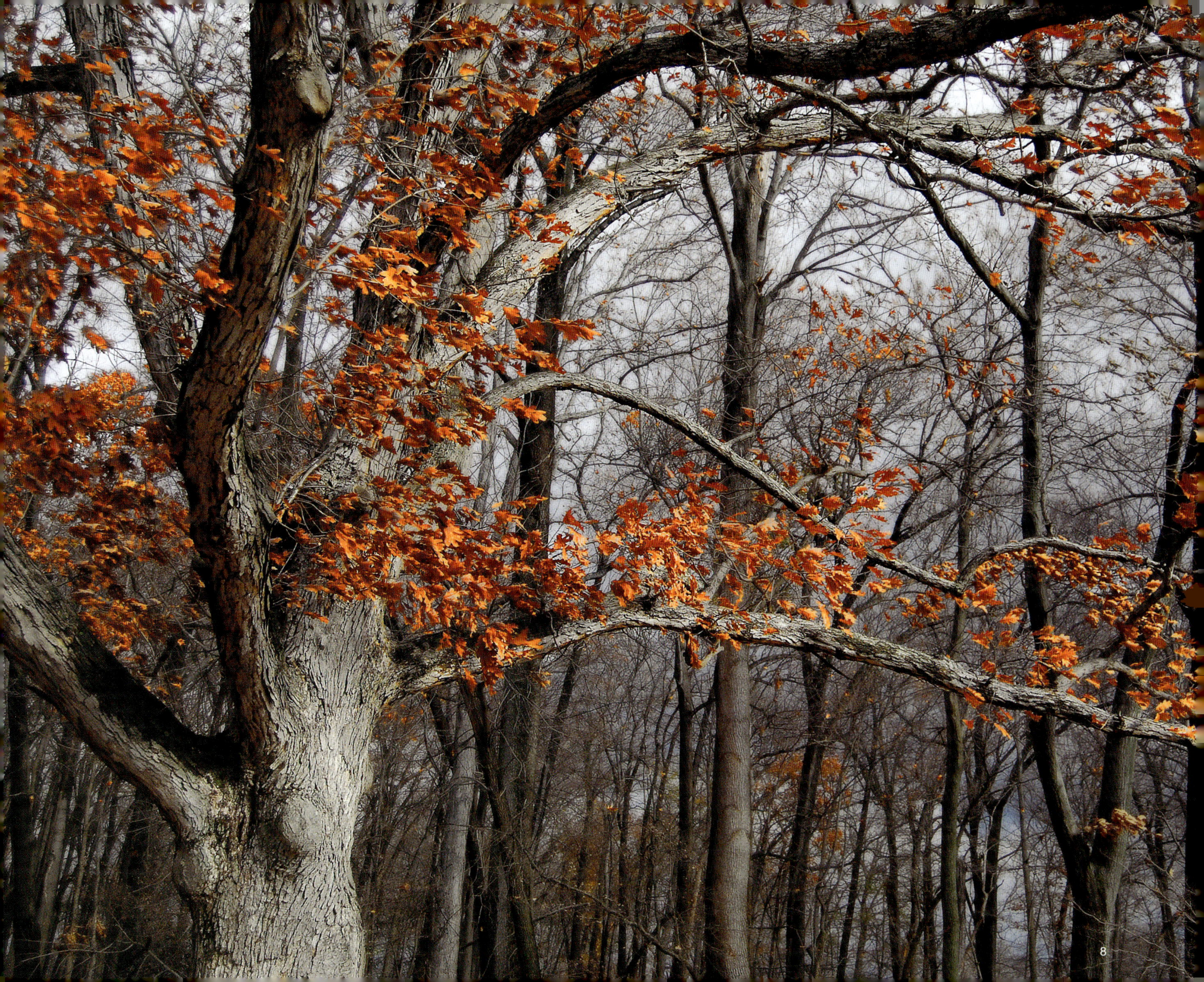

This is the monument of Anthony Wayne. It sits high on a hill overlooking the valley. The sun sets here and he has a front row seat. Very majestic.

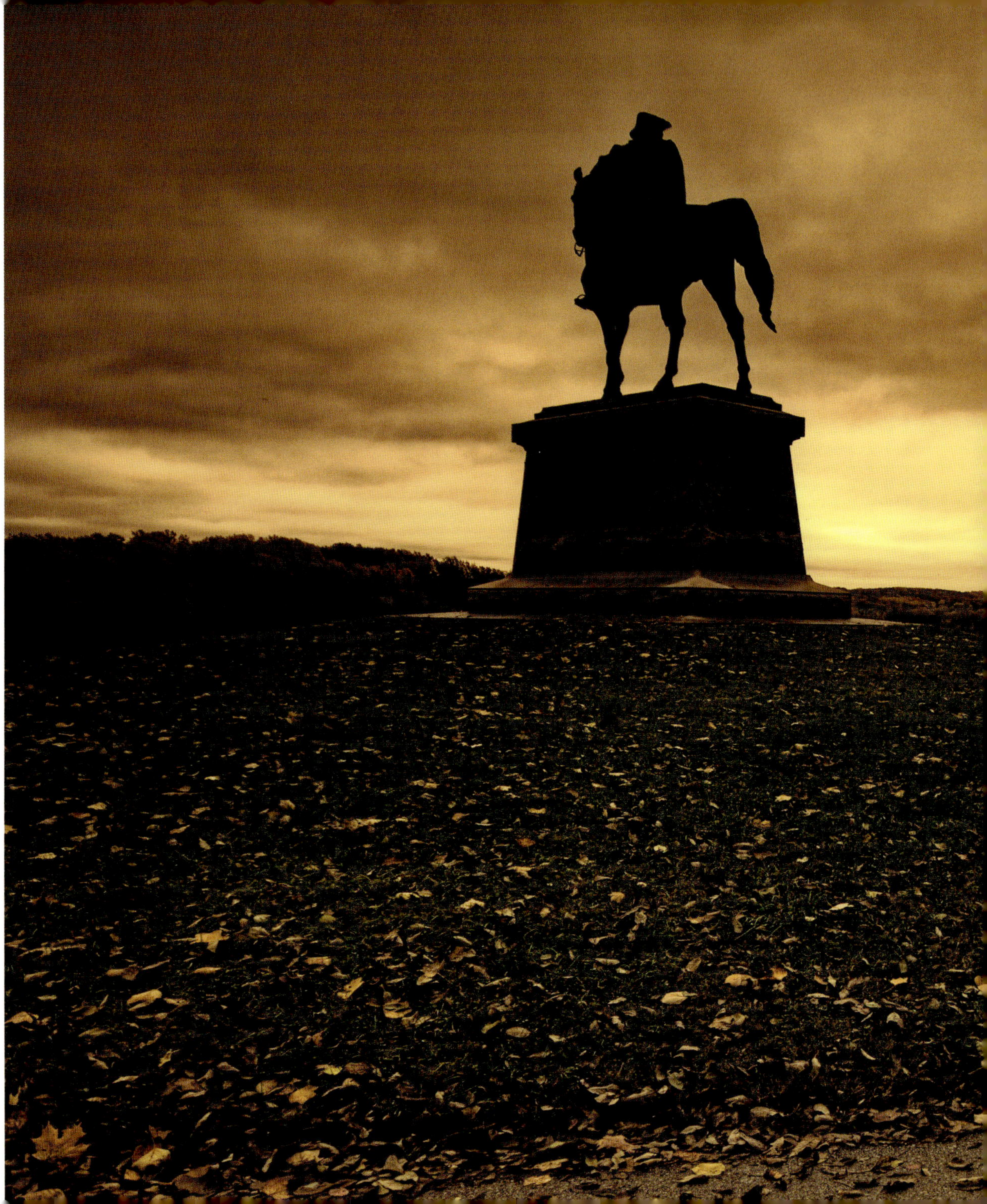

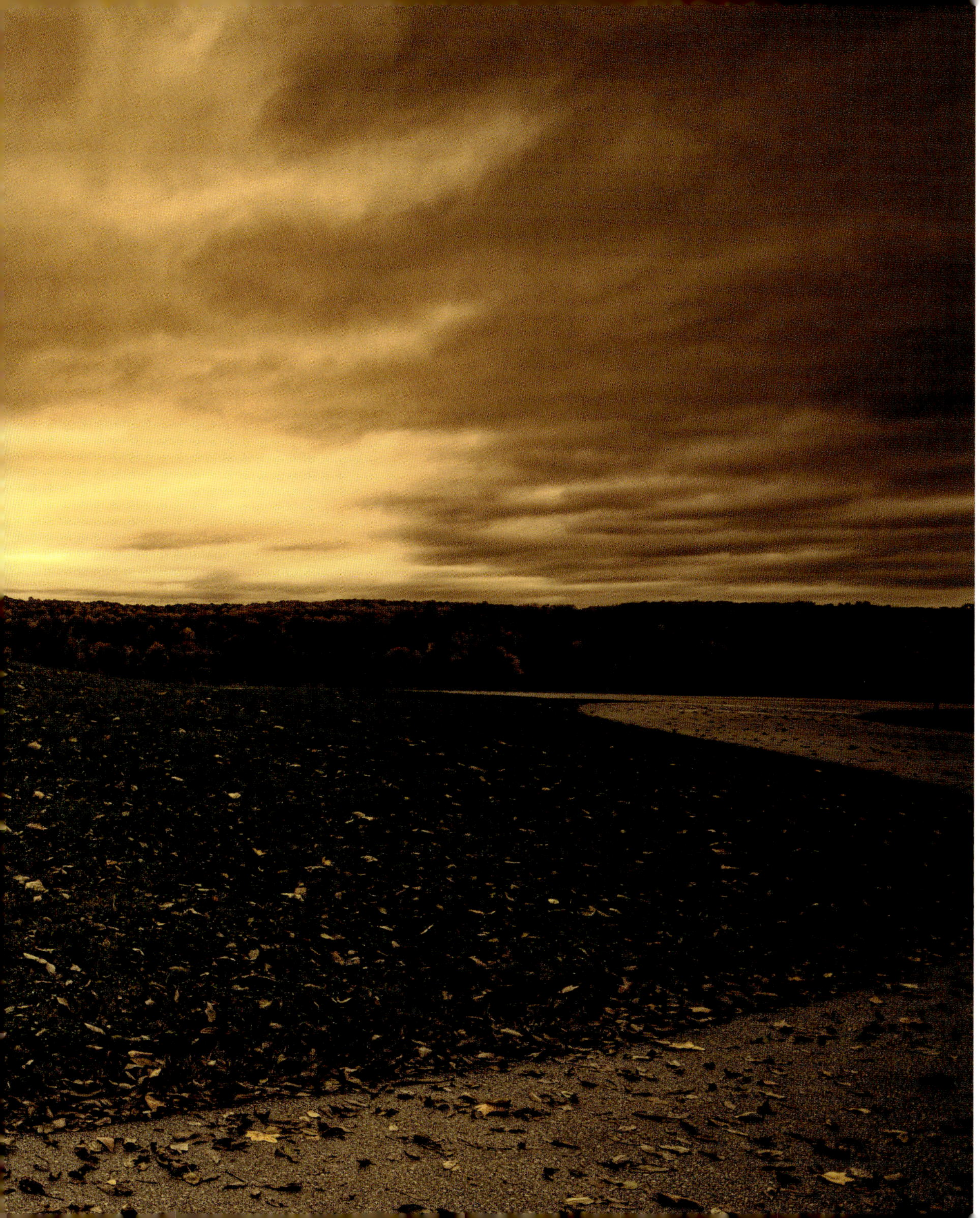

HISTORY LESSON #2:

ANTHONY WAYNE

Born in Pennsylvania in 1745, Wayne was a tanner by trade. He served as a member of the Pennsylvania legislature, and on the committee of safety. In 1776, he was appointed Colonel of the 4th Pennsylvania Battalion and sent on an arduous expedition to Canada. Because of his performance during this difficult campaign, he was promoted to Brigadier General and joined Washington at Morristown, New Jersey. He later returned as commander of the U.S. Army and opened the "Ohio Country."

Wayne was one of Washington's most aggressive subordinates. His nickname "Mad Anthony" is deceptive, as Wayne was not mentally unbalanced, but rather always wanted to be where the fight was.

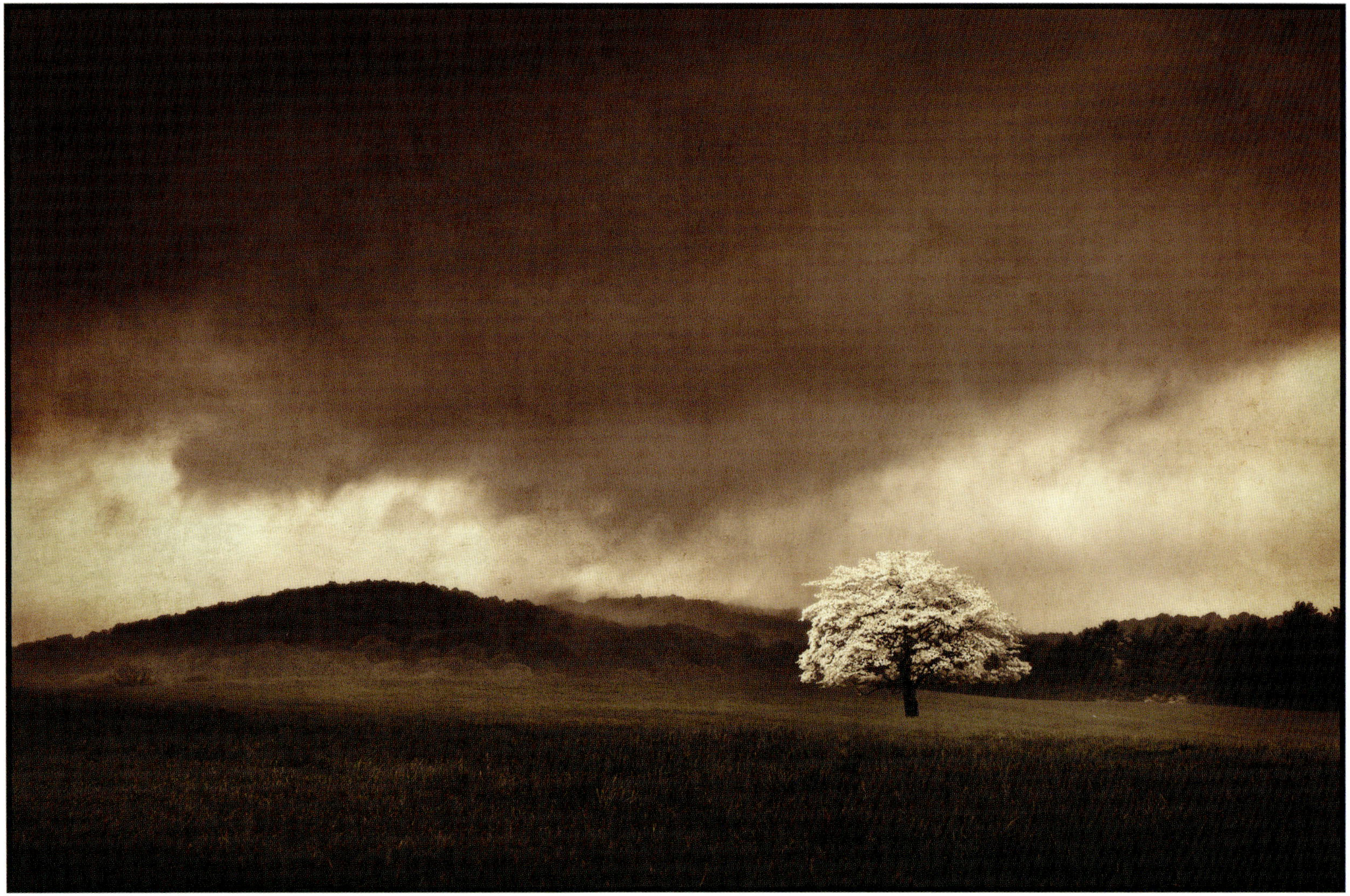

Some of the best times for making images are before, during, and after storms.
Above you can see the overhead threat and on the right, it's full-blown — literally.

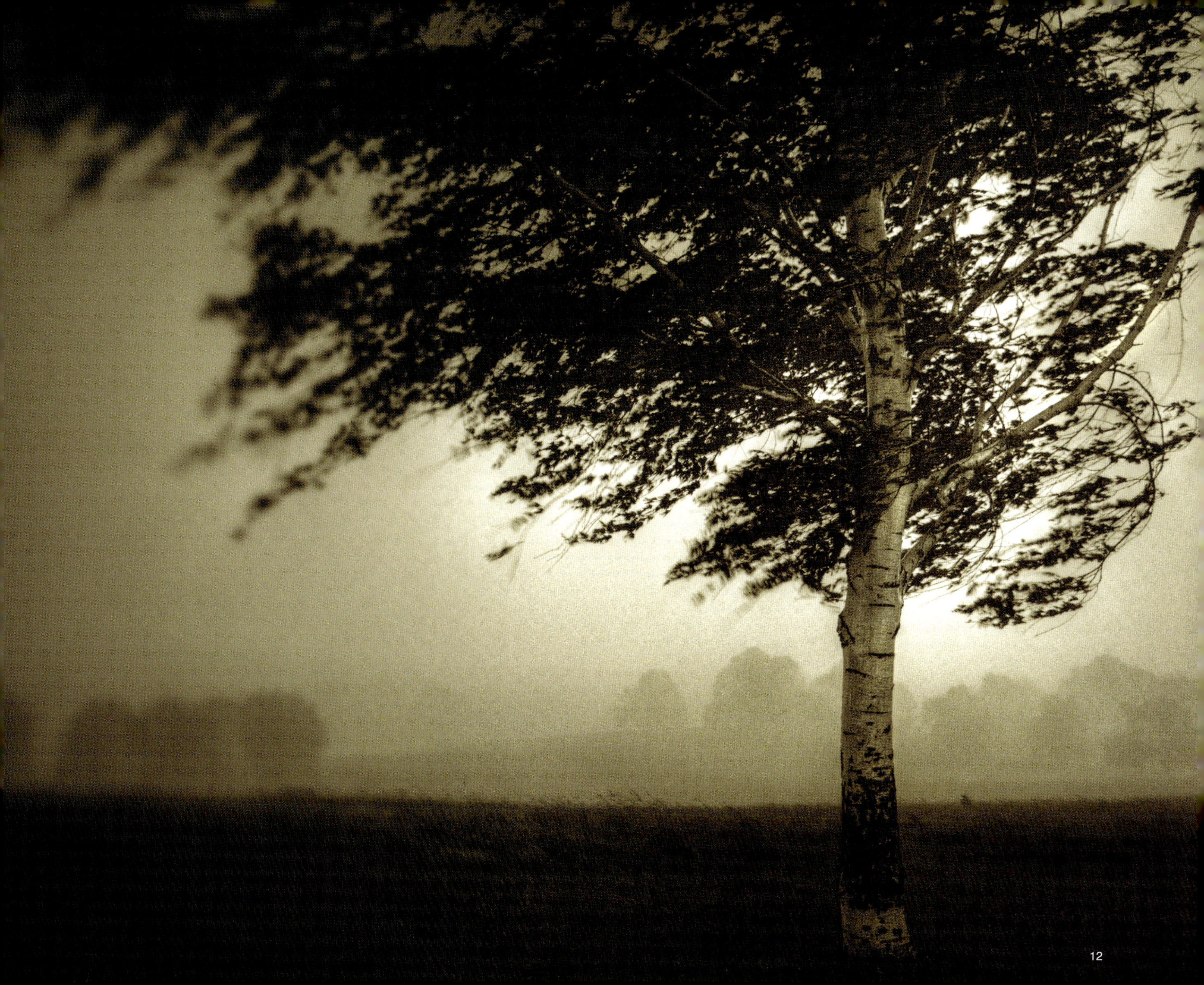

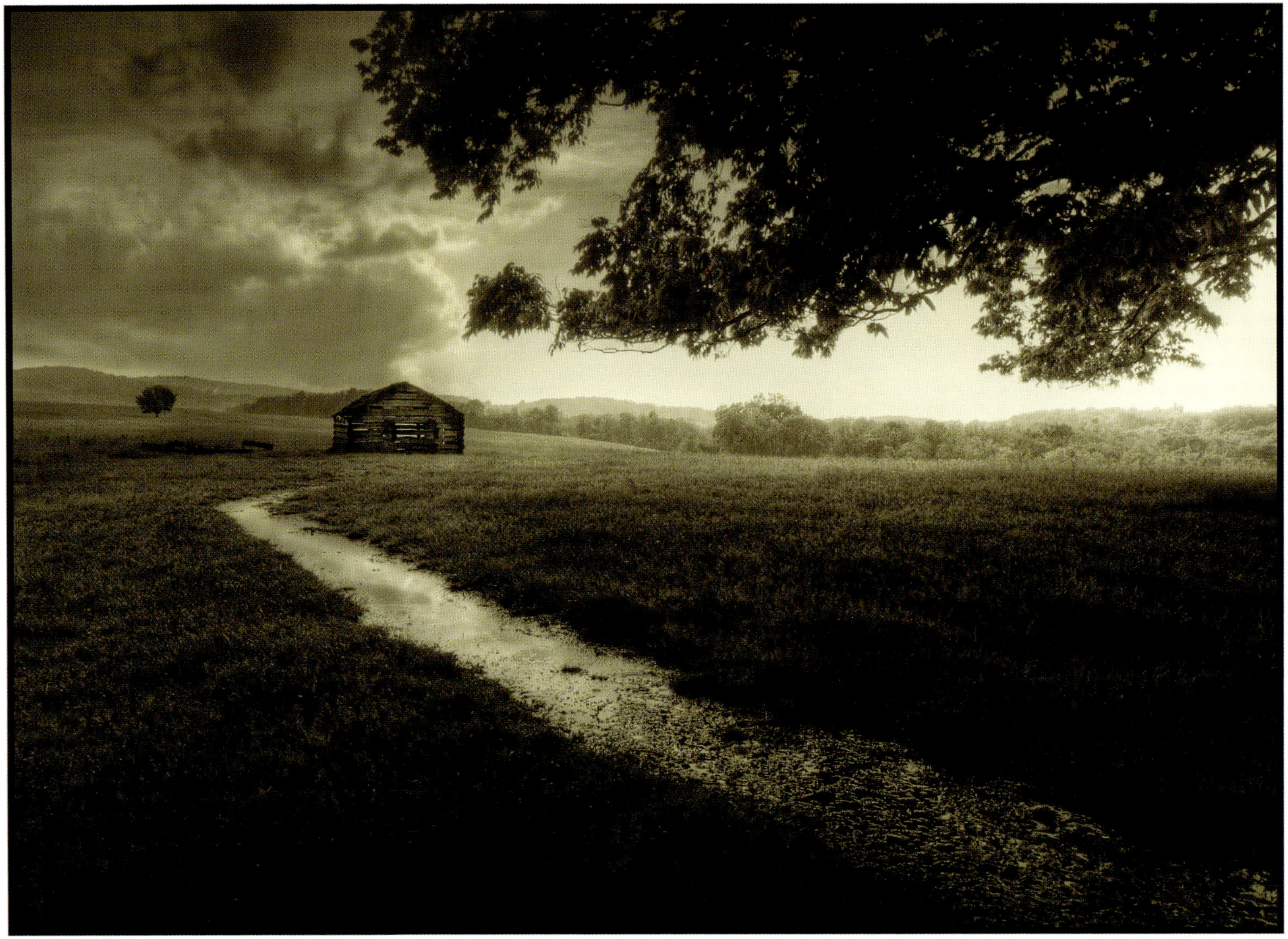

The aftermath of a summer storm leaves a mini-river flowing to a soldier's hut.
This is the area next to the Muhlenberg Brigade (opposite page), the first stop of the Valley Forge encampment tour.

HISTORY LESSON #3:

JOHN PETER GABRIEL MUHLENBERG

Muhlenberg was born in Pennsylvania, the son of a Lutheran missionary. He was educated in Germany, but became enamored with military life and joined the Royal American Regiment of the British Army and served with them until 1767. He then studied theology and became a pastor in the Shenandoah Valley of Virginia in 1772. In 1774, he served in the Virginia House of Burgesses and on the local Committee of Safety. He was appointed a Colonel in the Virginia militia in 1775 and in 1776 became Colonel of the 8th Virginia Regiment, or German Regiment, composed of German Americans from Pennsylvania and Maryland. In February of 1777, he was promoted to Brigadier General and sent north, where he showed excellent military ability and participated in most major actions. He commanded a Brigade at Valley Forge, and was transferred to Virginia in March of 1780. He commanded a brigade of Light Infantry at Yorktown. Muhlenberg was breveted a Major General just before his retirement in November 1783.

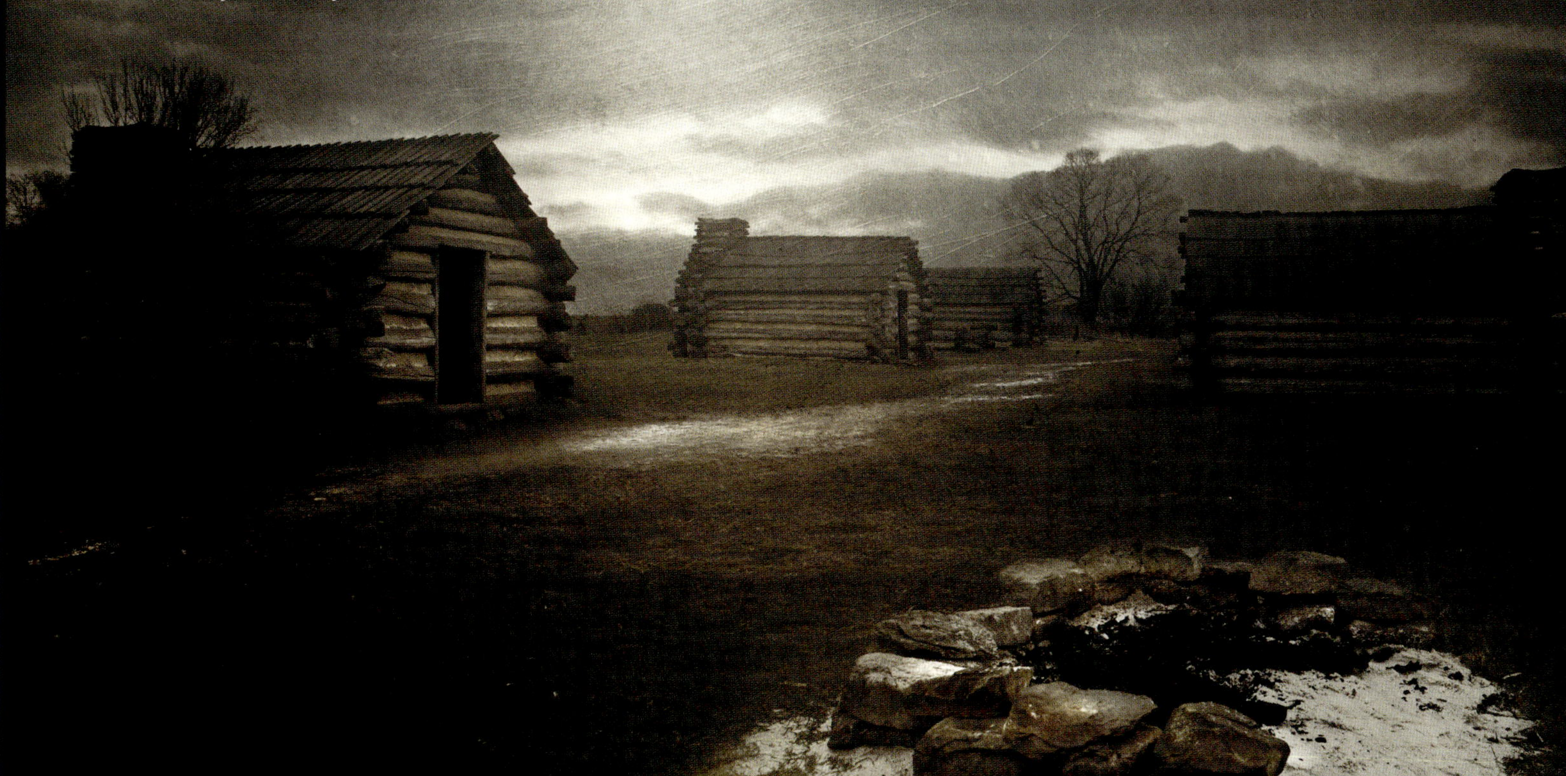

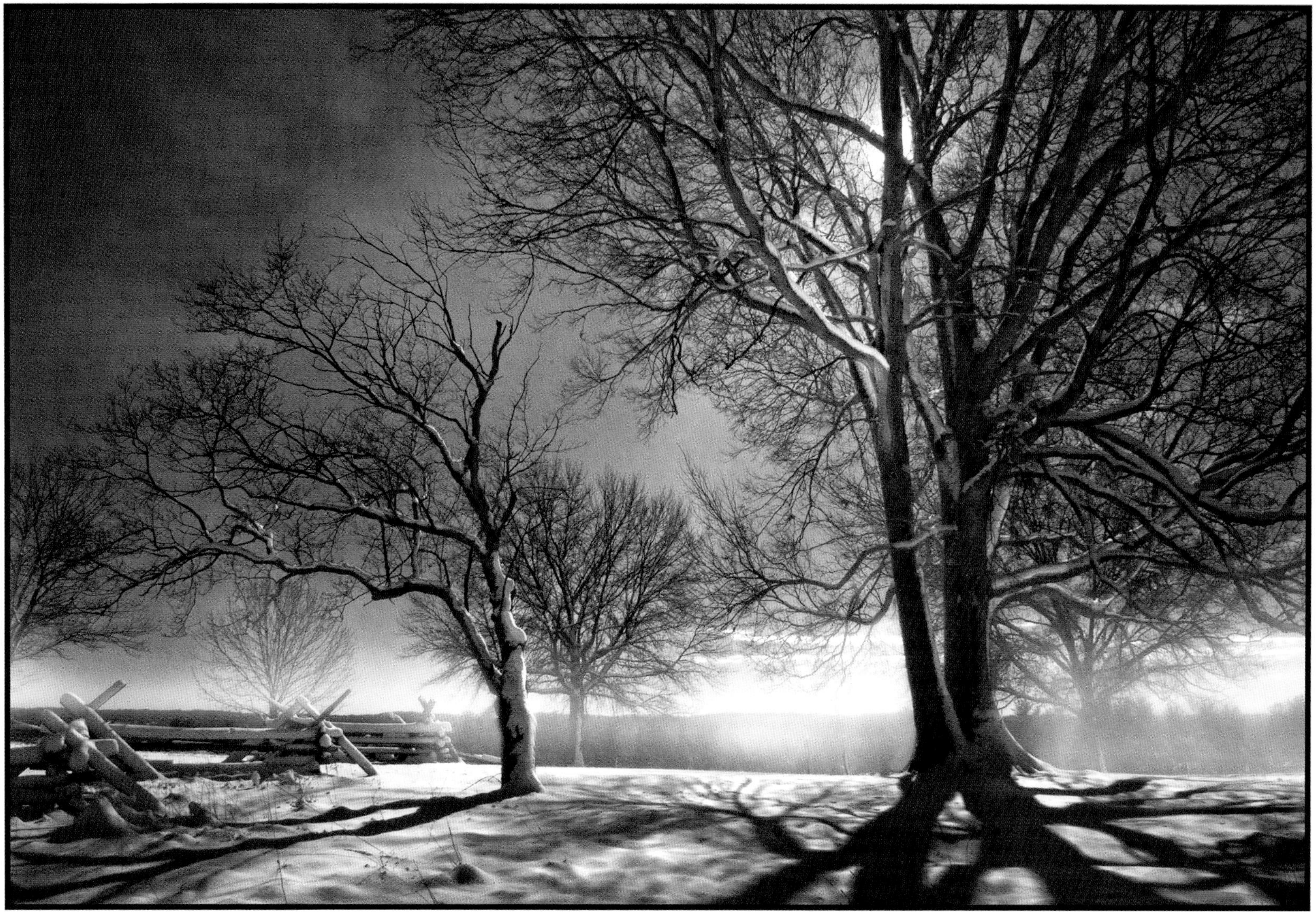

Sometimes the wind and snow can whip around and freeze you to the bone...

This was shot at Muhlenberg Brigade.

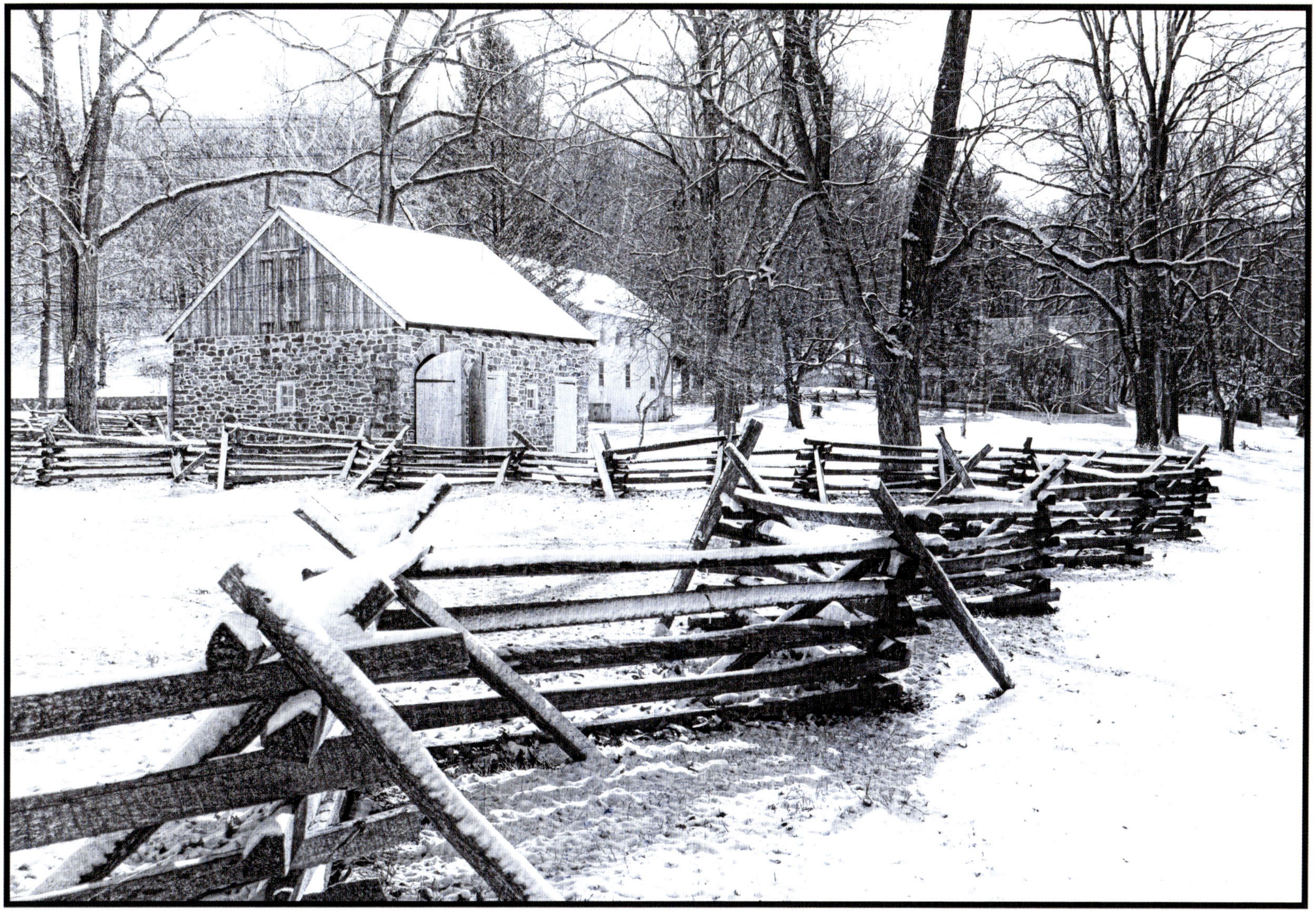

...but in a soft, falling snow it is quiet and very peaceful.

This is the barn in the area adjacent to Washington's Headquarters.

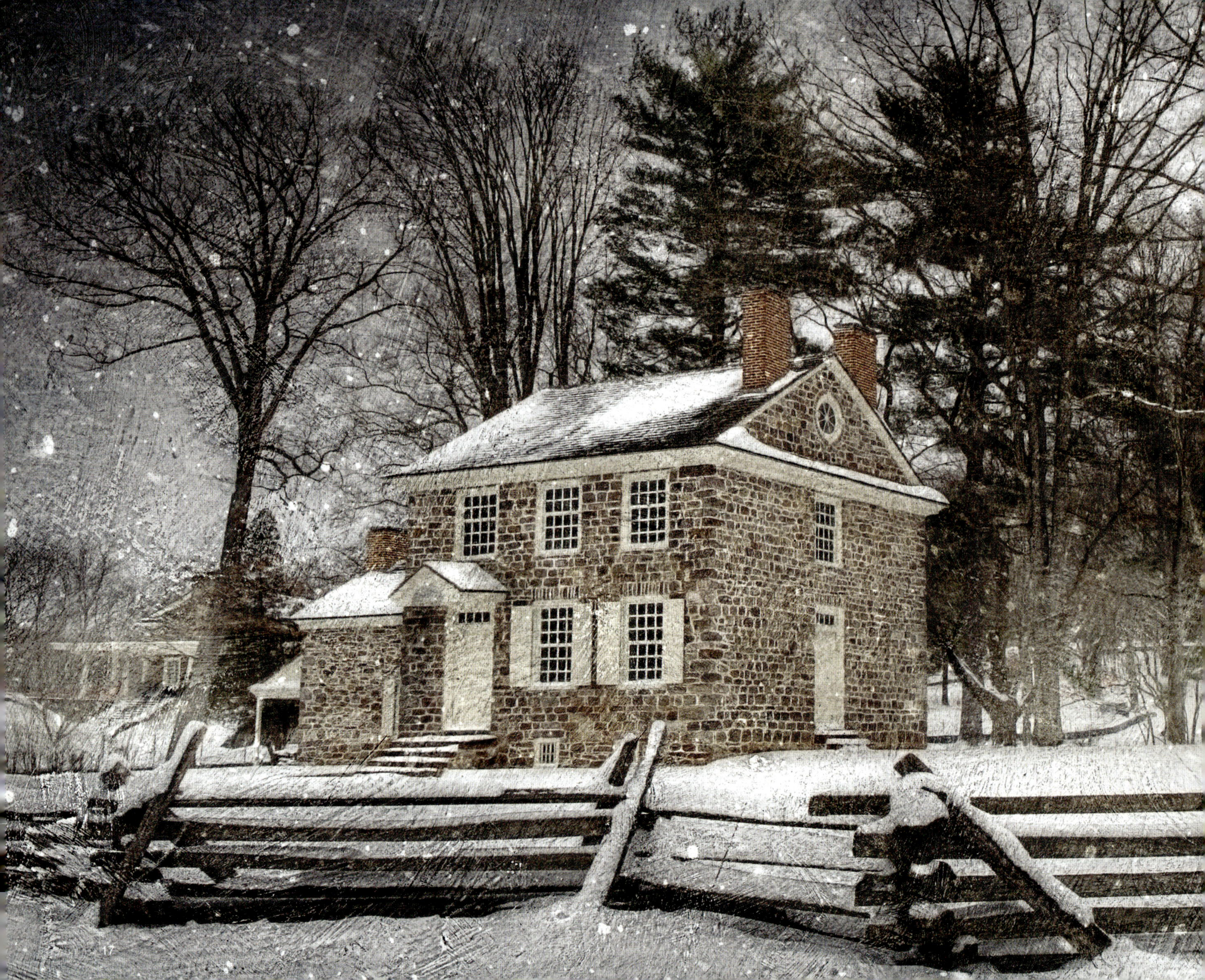

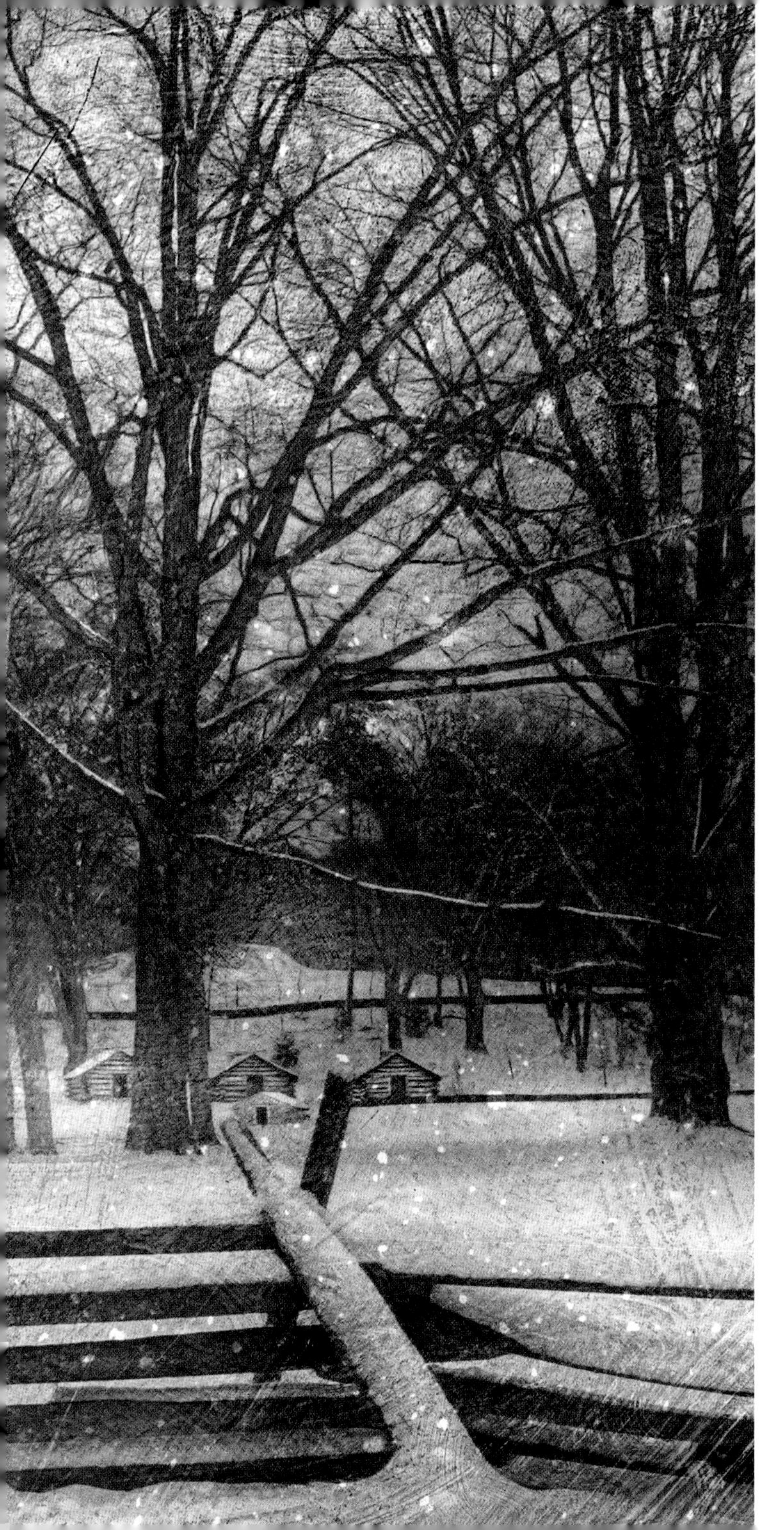

HISTORY LESSON #4:
WASHINGTON'S HEADQUARTERS

General Washington rented this house from its occupant, Mrs. Deborah Hewes. The property was owned by Isaac Potts. It was here that the General and his staff would organize and orchestrate plans for the Continental Army at Valley Forge, as well as the troops in the newly-formed states to the north and south of the encampment.

Through the winter of 1777 and spring of 1778, many of the General's Officers shared or rented local farm houses in the area. The majority of the soldiers, however, built and lived in huts.

Most of the structure that is standing today is original, including the handrail leading to the upstairs rooms. So, if you visit, be sure to walk up the stairs and take history by the hand.

You can not do a portrait of Valley Forge without its cornerstone,
the Headquarters of General Washington and his staff.

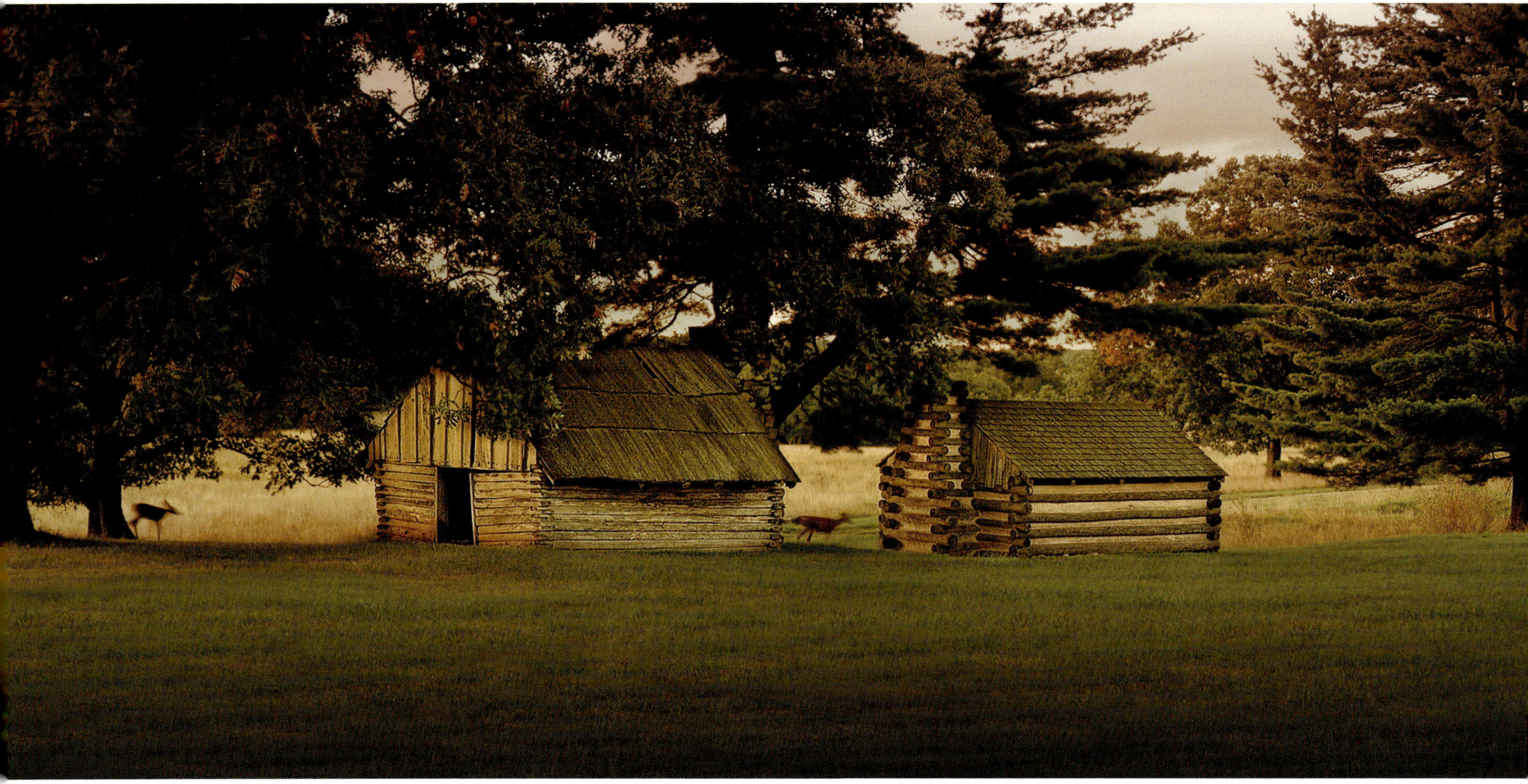

These are two of the soldier huts in Conway's Brigade. It's a panoramic image consisting of eight vertical shots that have been digitally "stitched" together. The deer in motion were a bonus.

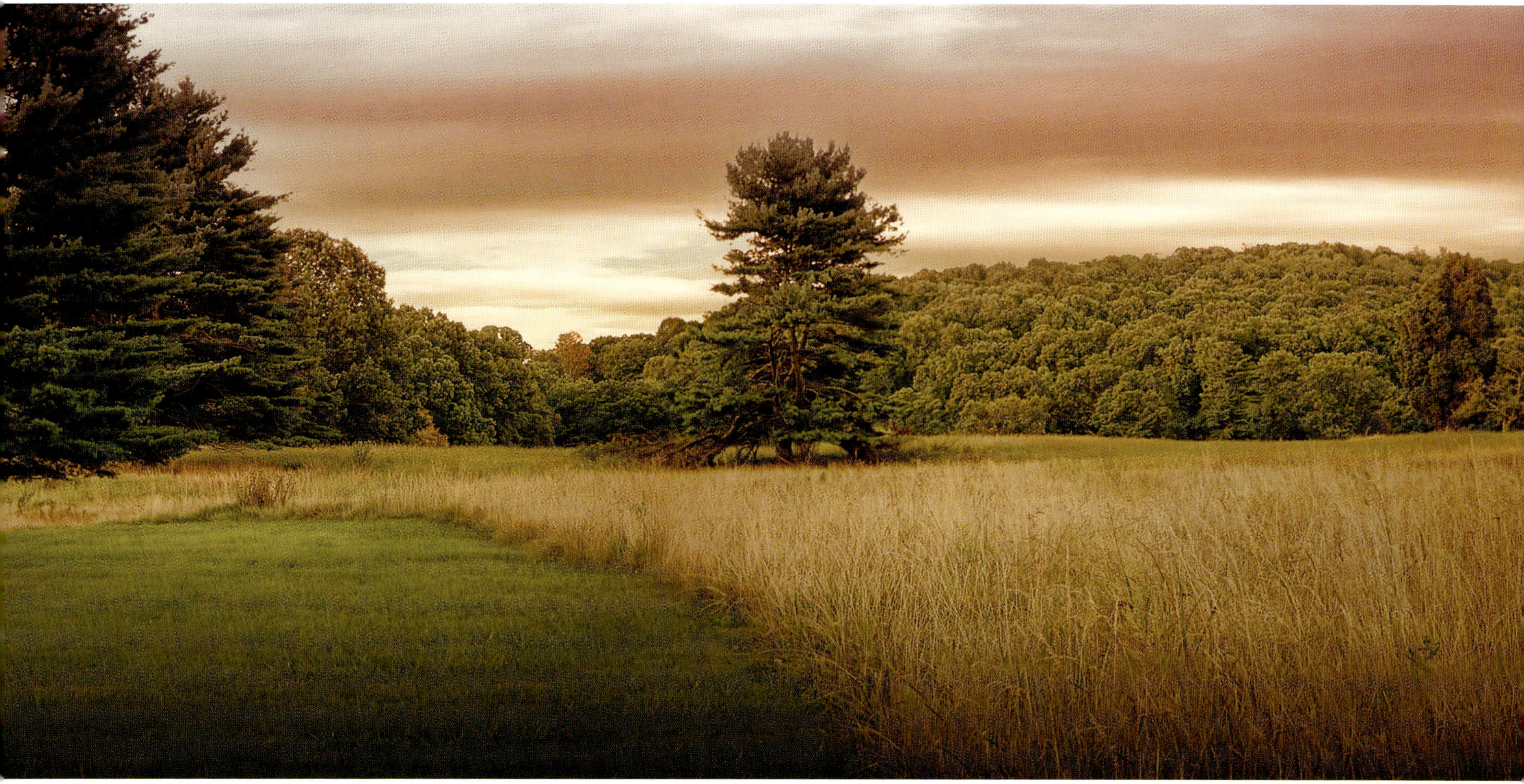

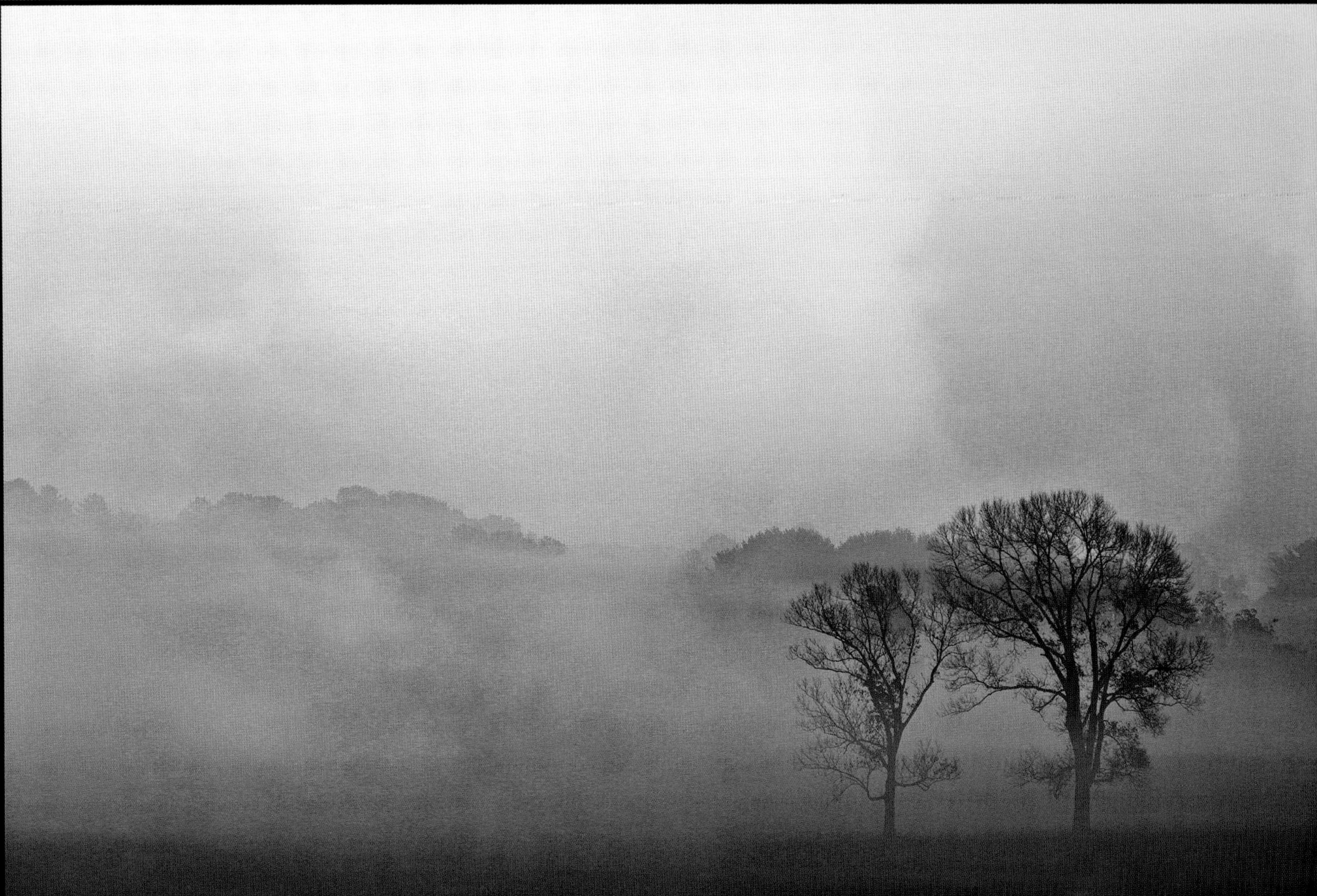

These are two of the many trees in an area called the Grand Parade Ground. It is a large low-lying section of the park and is a great basin for fog. It's located near the statue of General von Steuben.

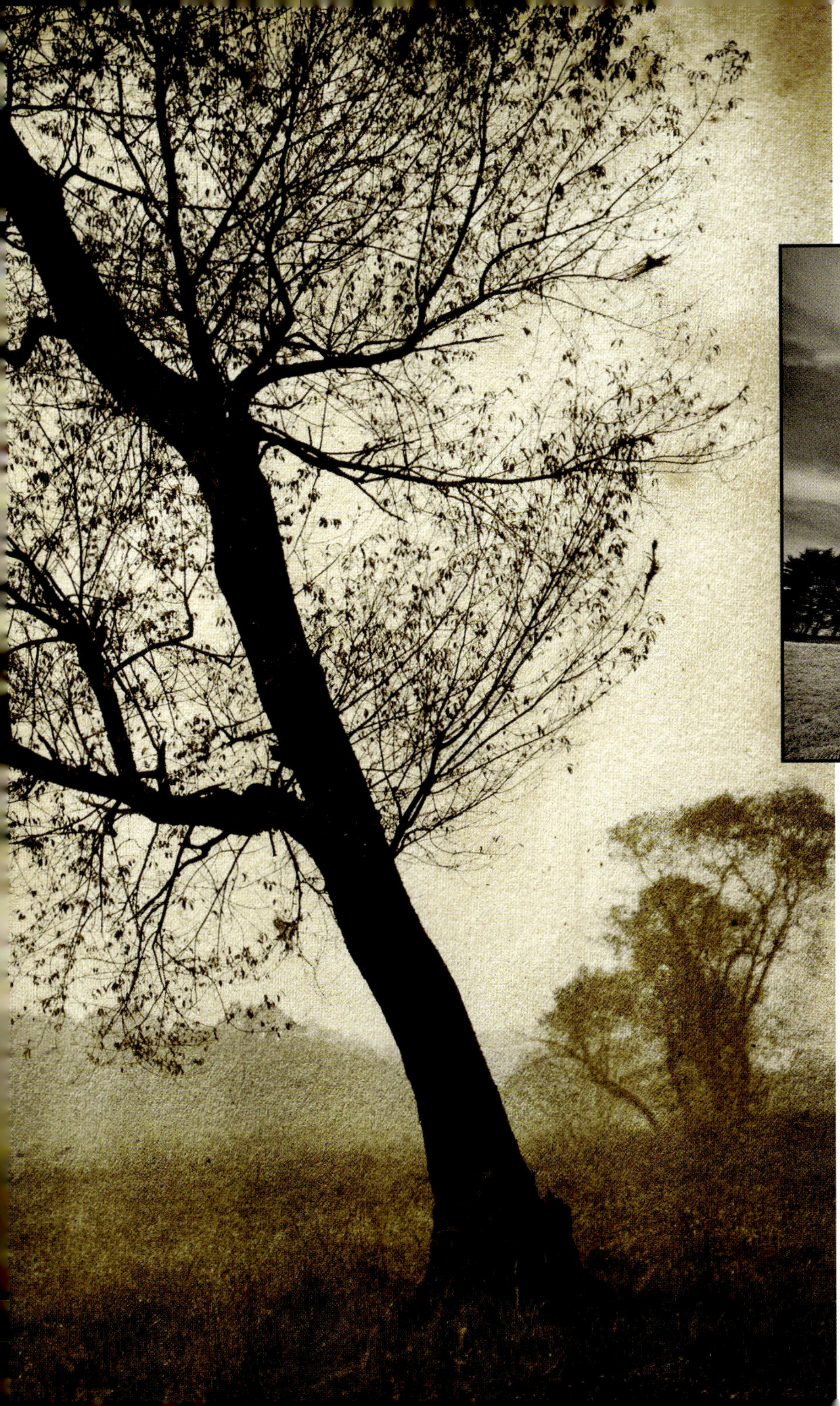

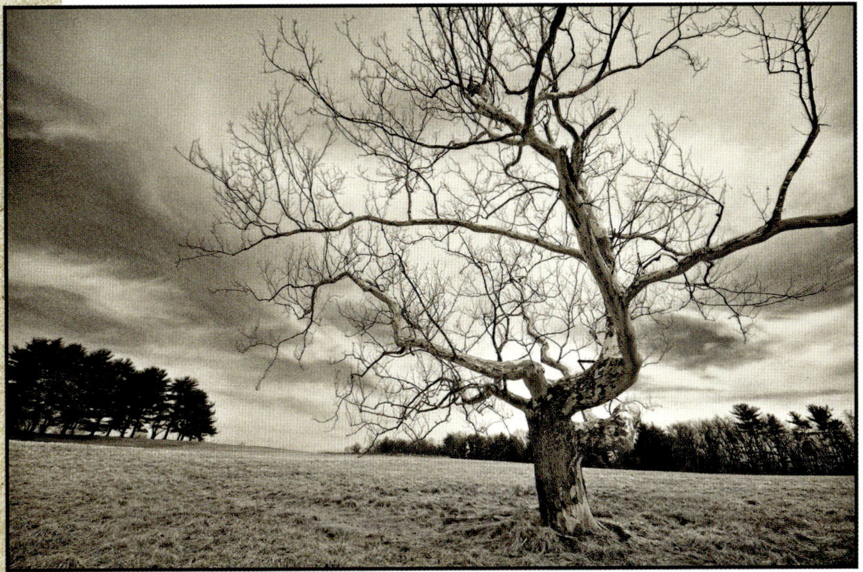

HISTORY LESSON 5:

THE GRAND PARADE GROUND

At the center of the encampment is the Grand Parade Ground. It is a massive area that General von Steuben used to drill brigades. He sent the troops over this rough terrain in simulated battle to better prepare them for the enemy encounters that lay ahead.

On a soft, misty, early morning, if you listen closely, you can still hear echoes of General von Steuben.

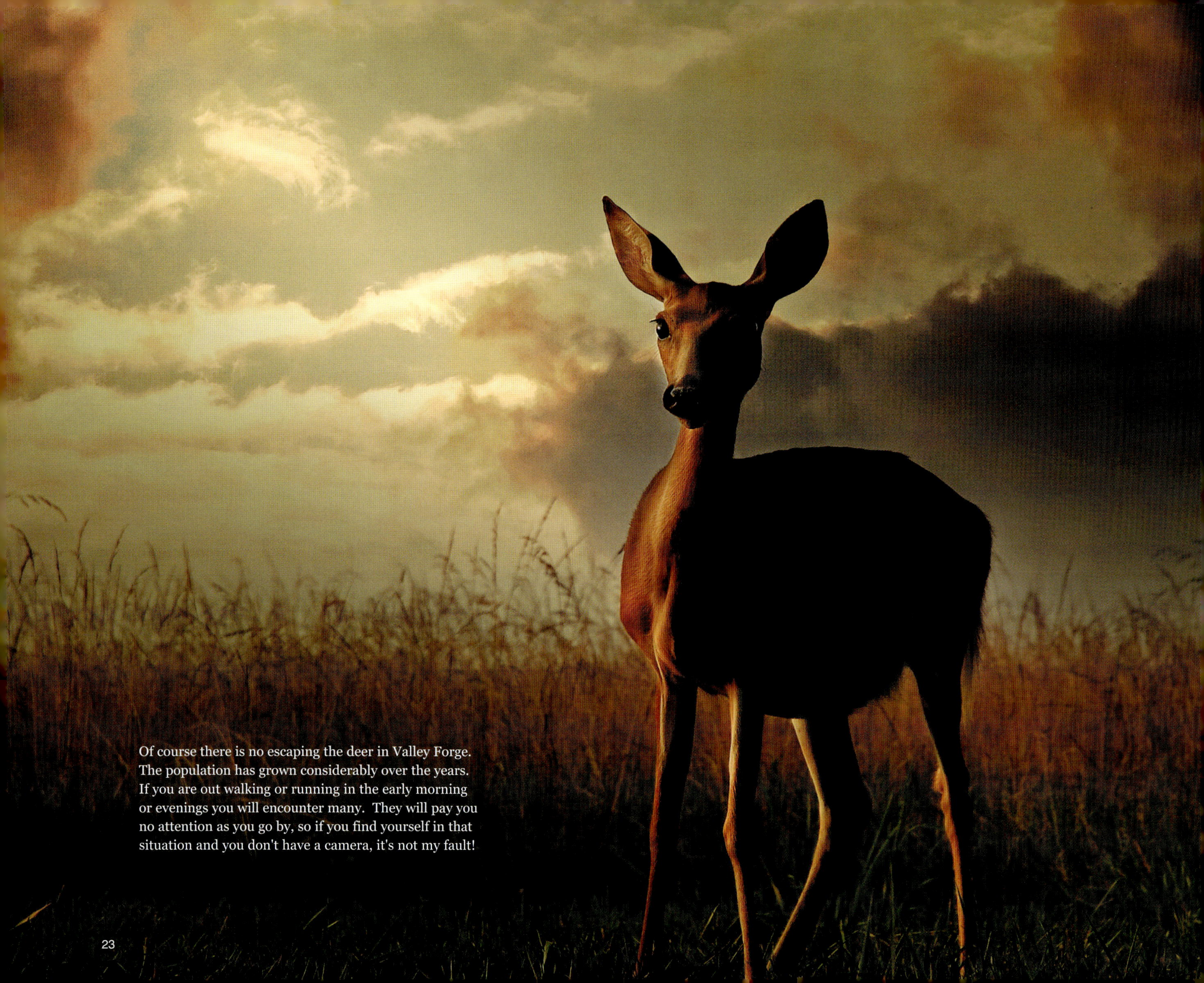

Of course there is no escaping the deer in Valley Forge. The population has grown considerably over the years. If you are out walking or running in the early morning or evenings you will encounter many. They will pay you no attention as you go by, so if you find yourself in that situation and you don't have a camera, it's not my fault!

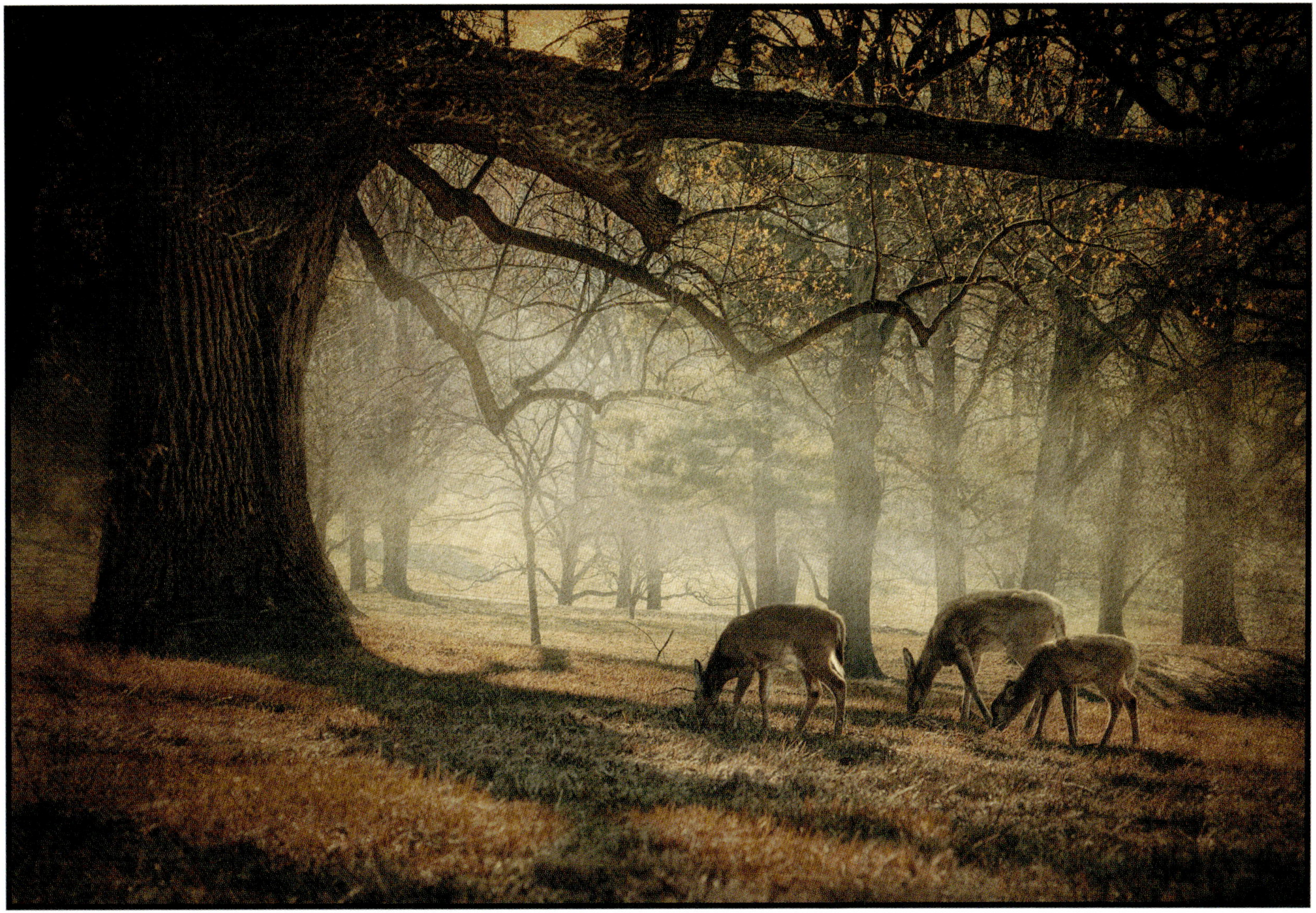

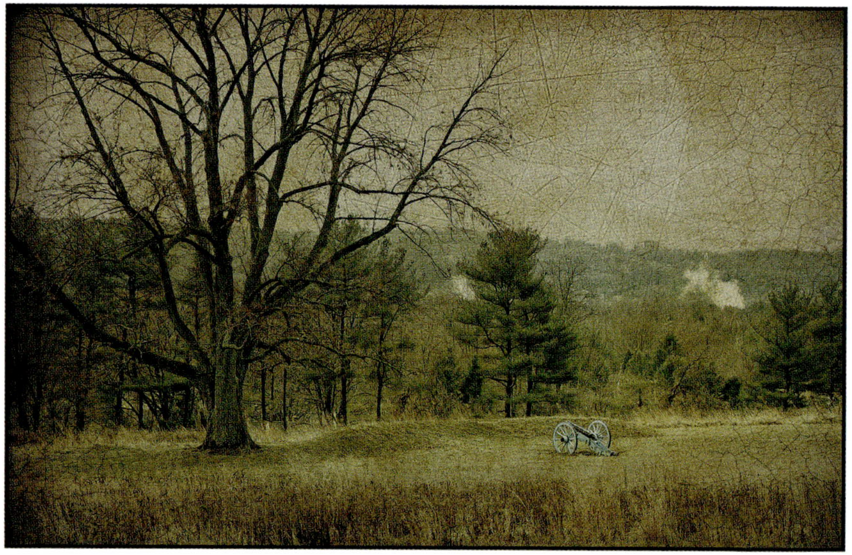

A common misconception about Valley Forge is that a battle was fought there. Sorry, no battle. It was strictly an encampment for our young soldiers to prepare for what was ahead.

While there were no battles fought at Valley Forge, there was a need to be prepared for one. You will therefore find cannons positioned in key locations and almost always behind, or next to, a redoubt or redan. If you are like me and wondering what a redoubt or redan is, see the next page.

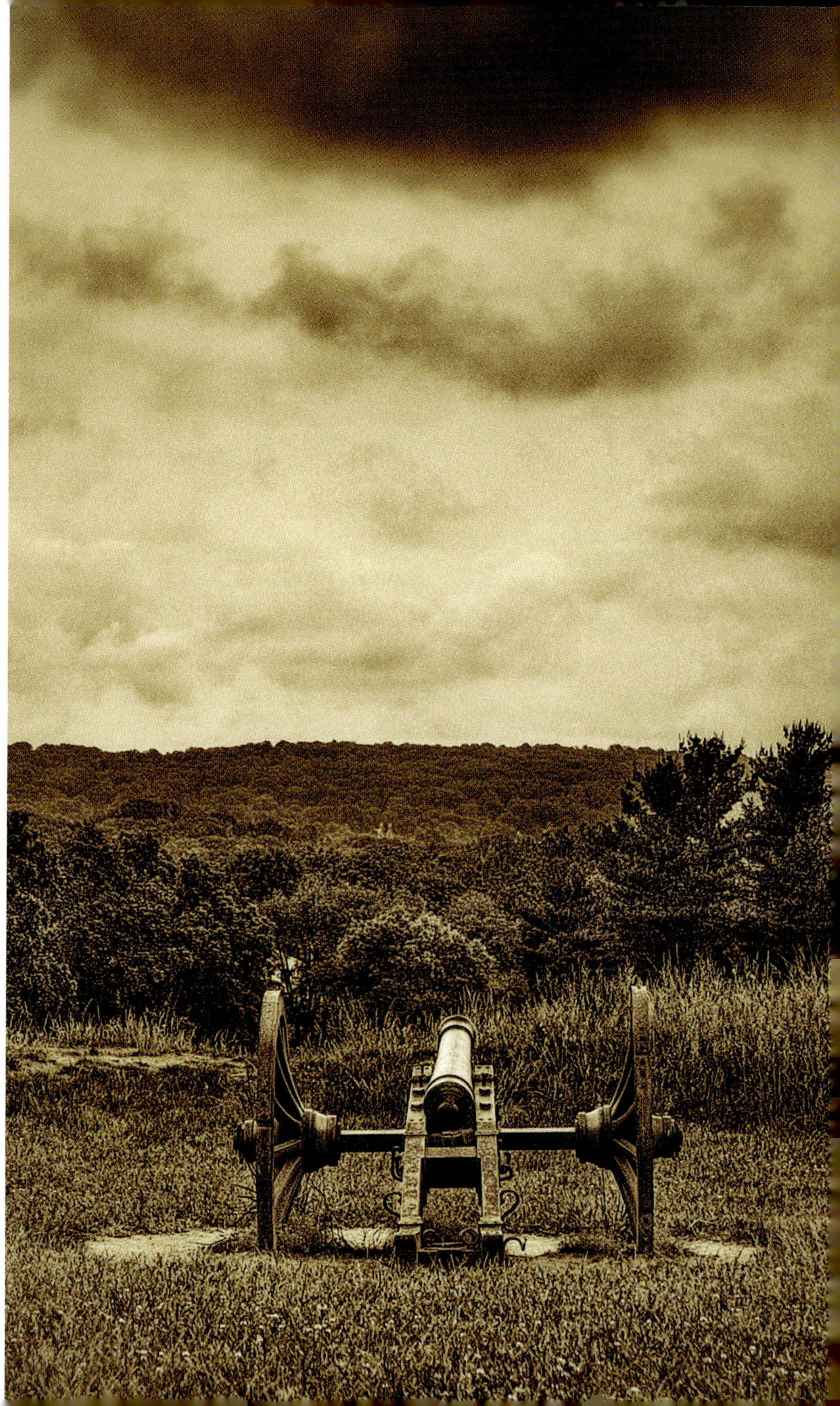

A redoubt is an enclosed defensive emplacement built to protect soldiers outside the main line of defense. Made of earth or, less commonly, stone, a redoubt can be a permanent structure or a quickly-constructed, temporary fortification. During the 18th century, redoubts were known to be part of the military strategies of most European empires.

A redan is much the same as a redoubt except the rear is open. A redoubt is enclosed on all four sides.

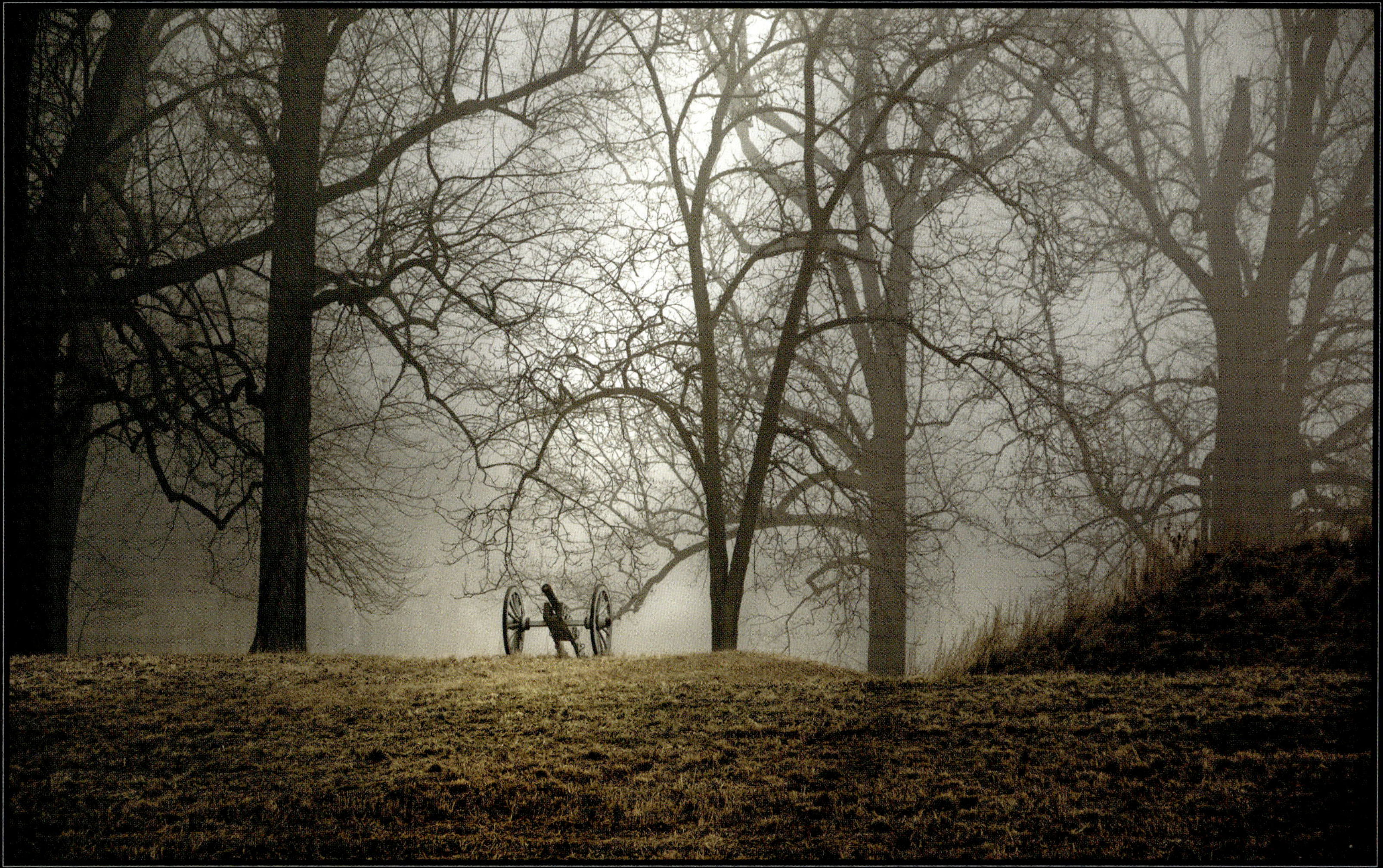

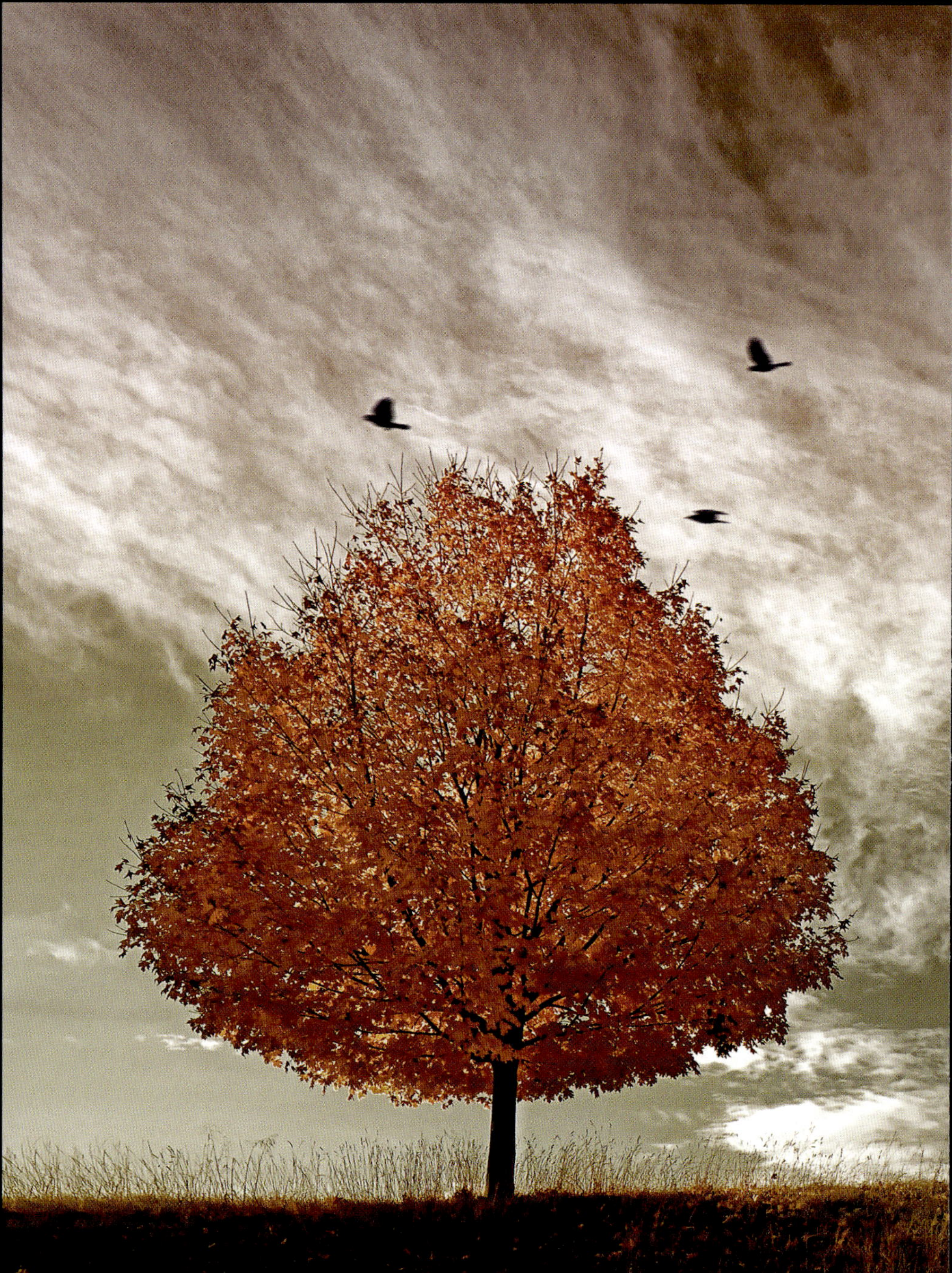

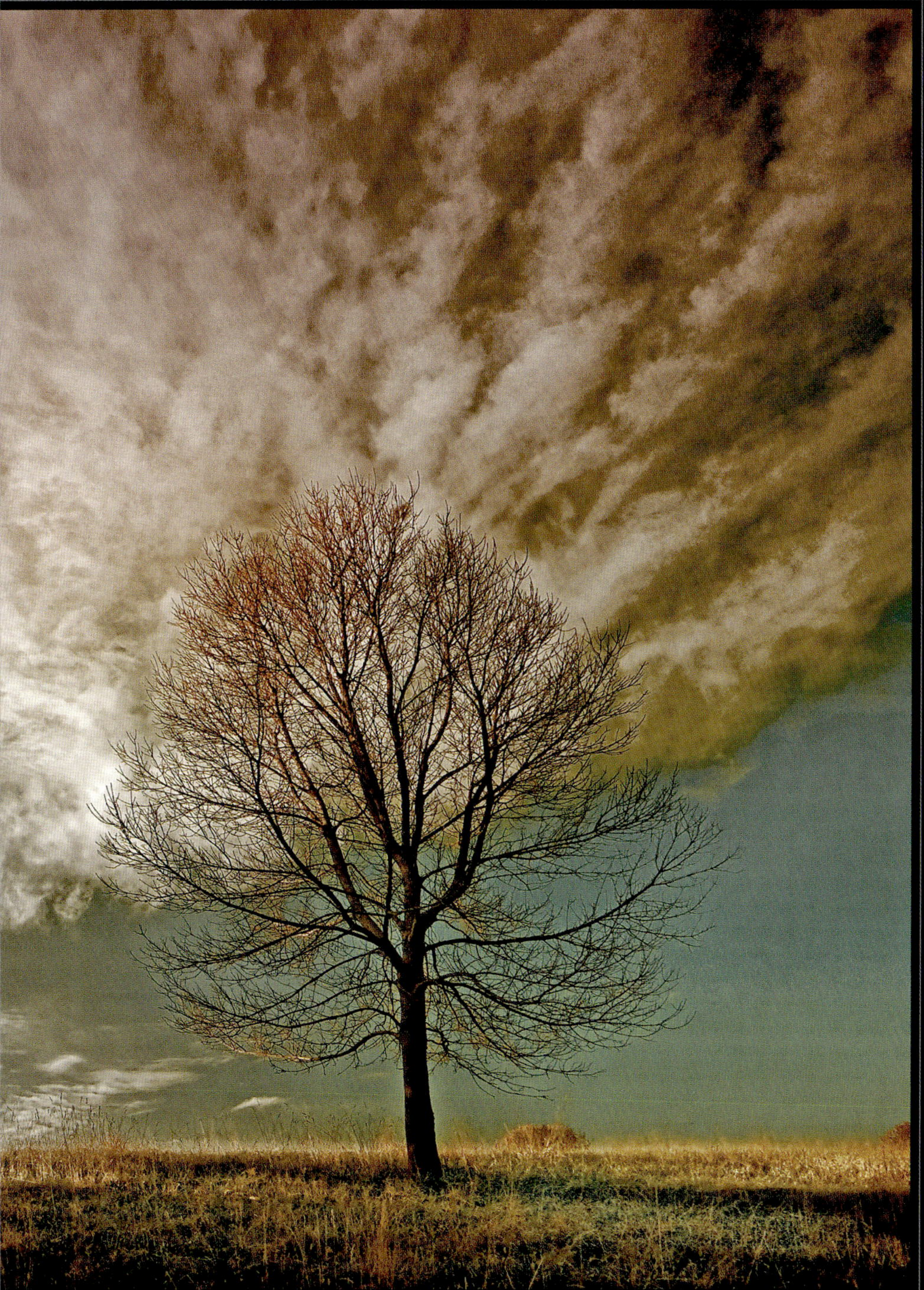

...The Have Nots.

Contemporary Valley Forge has many unique imaging opportunities. This is an example. I have been asked how I removed the leaves on the tree on the right. The answer is I didn't. These two exist side by side on a dead-end road near the Visitor Center.
The tree on the right is dead and has not had leaves in a while.

I discovered this scene in the summer, but waited until Autumn to photograph and make the image.

"The Haves and the Have Nots" seemed like an appropriate title.

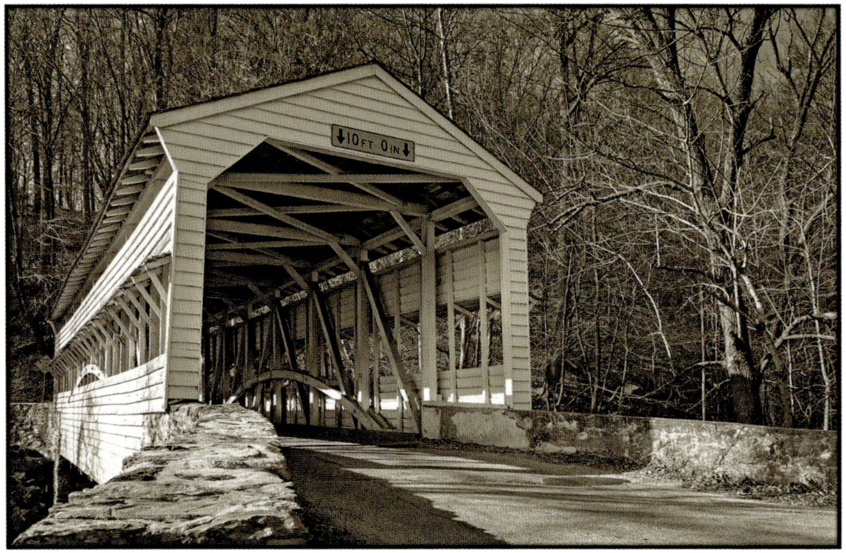

This is the Knox Covered Bridge located along Rt. 252 and Yellow Springs Road. It spans Valley Creek and was built in 1865. It is one of the few remaining covered bridges of Chester County. One of my European contacts asked why the bridge was covered. I didn't know at the time but later found out it was to protect the wooden bridge surface from the elements. It has been the subject of many paintings over the years.

Very scenic, indeed.

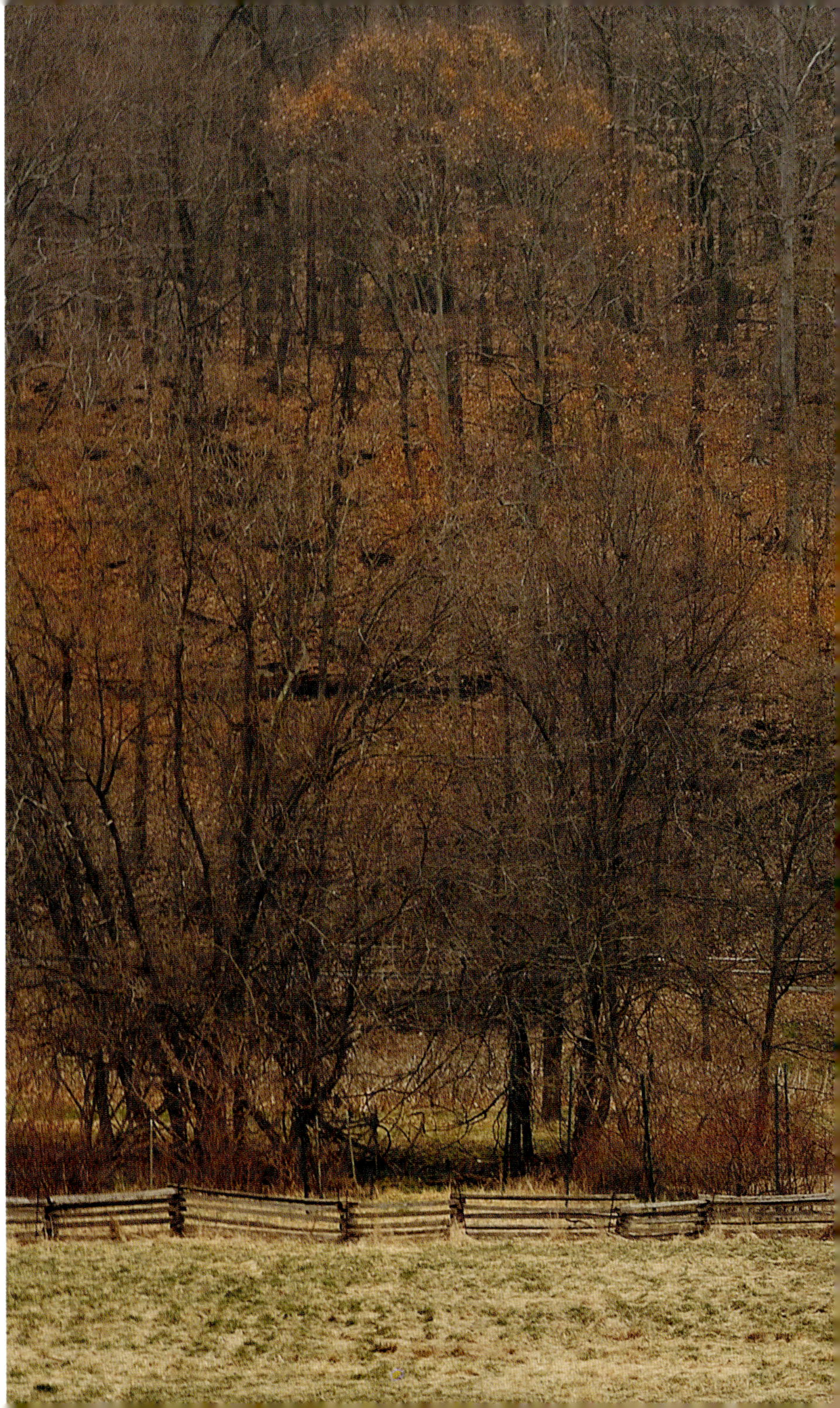

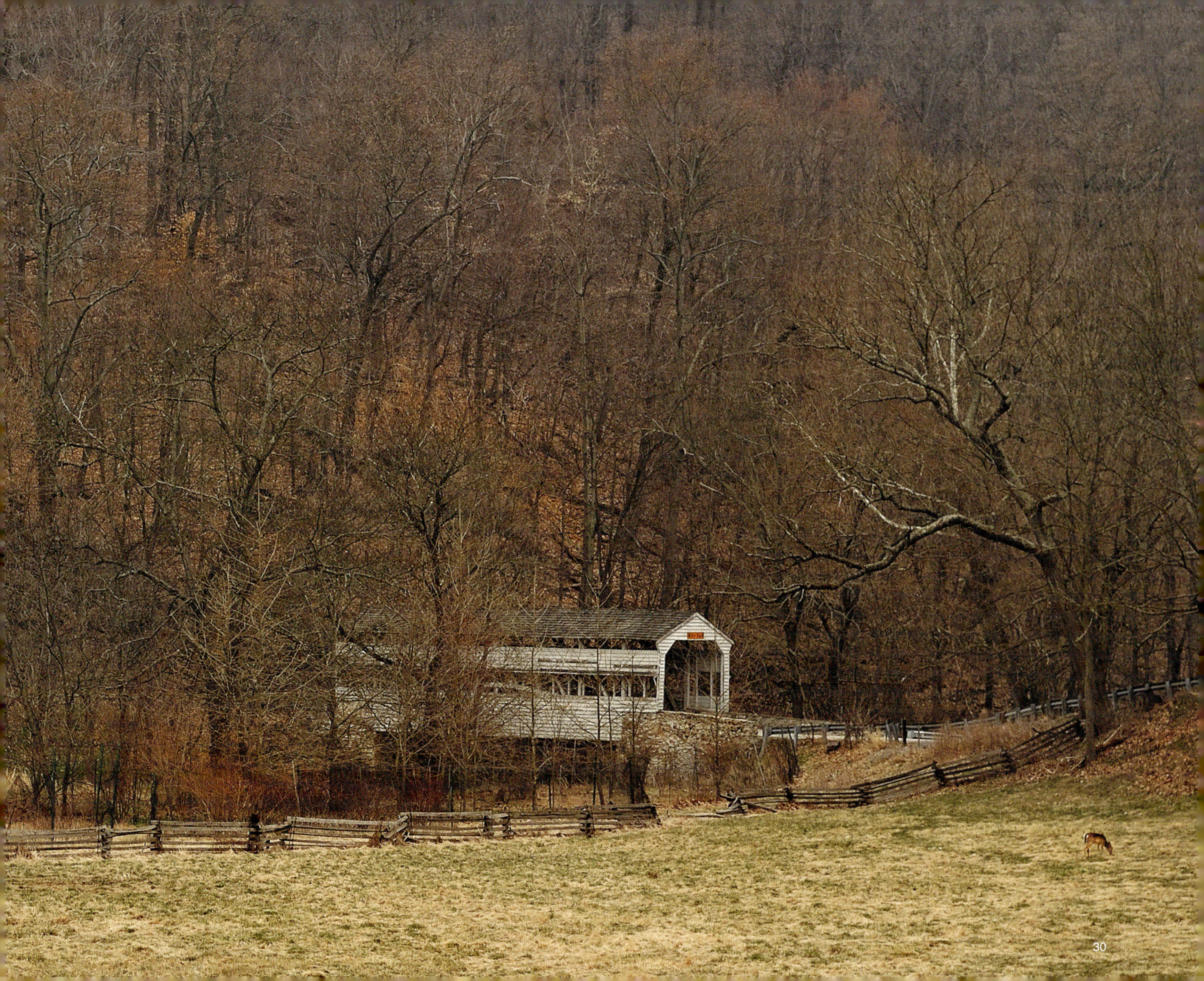

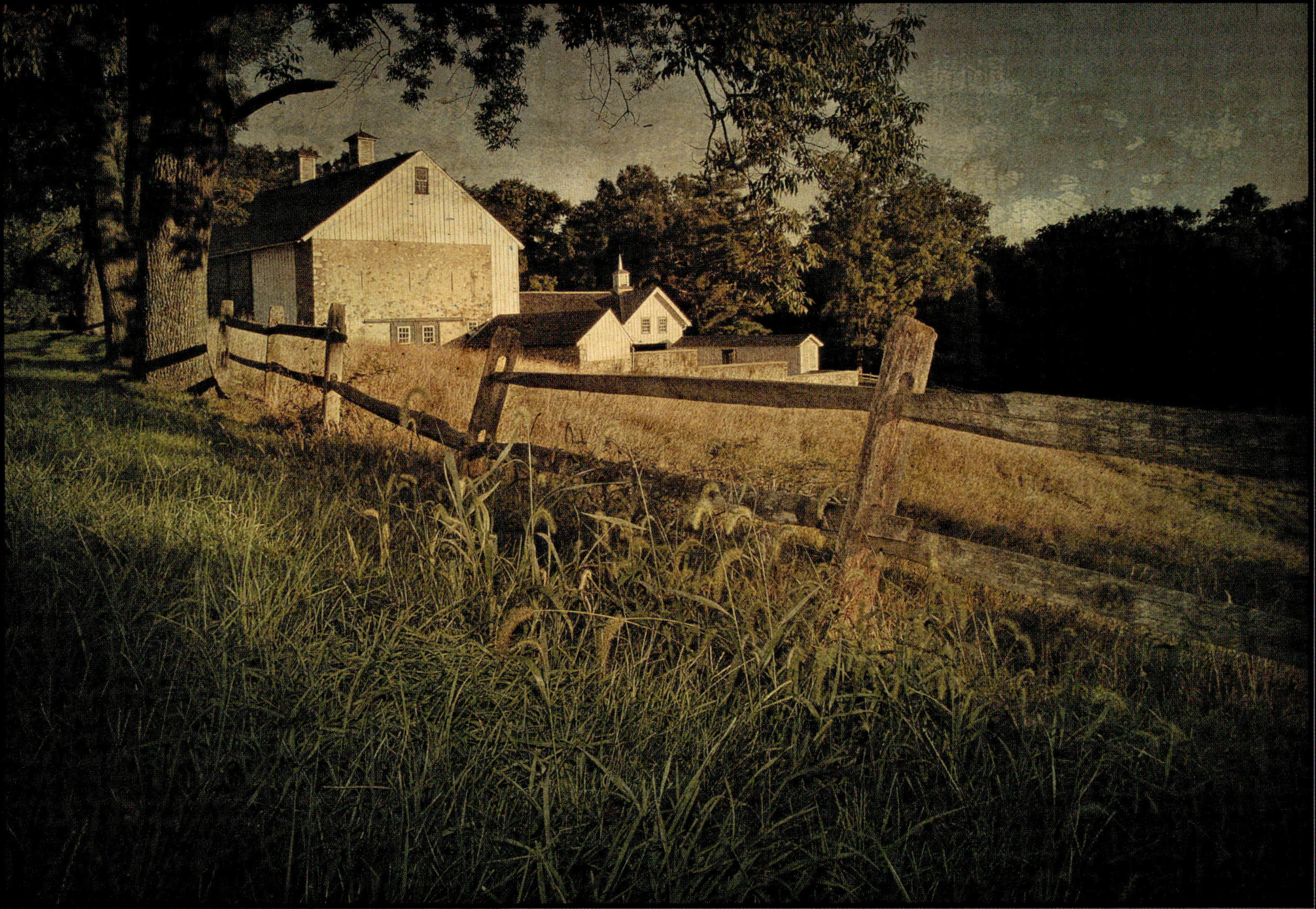

Another scenic place along Rt.252 is the Knox property.
On this side you get the warm glow of the evening sun setting,
and on the other side beautiful golden early morning light.

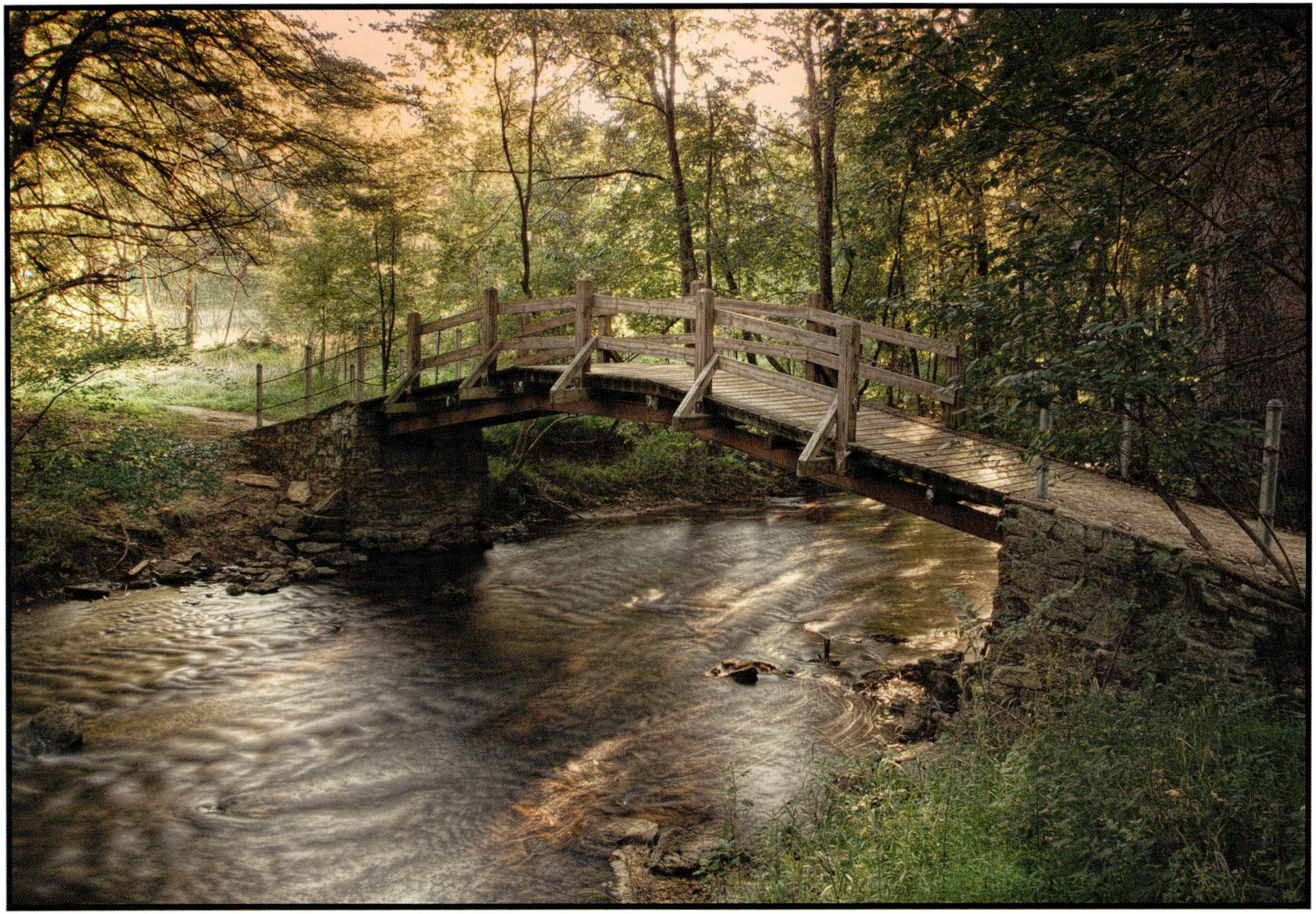

This is a foot bridge behind the Knox property.
It crosses Valley Creek just up-stream from the Covered Bridge.
I like to sit here and listen to the water.

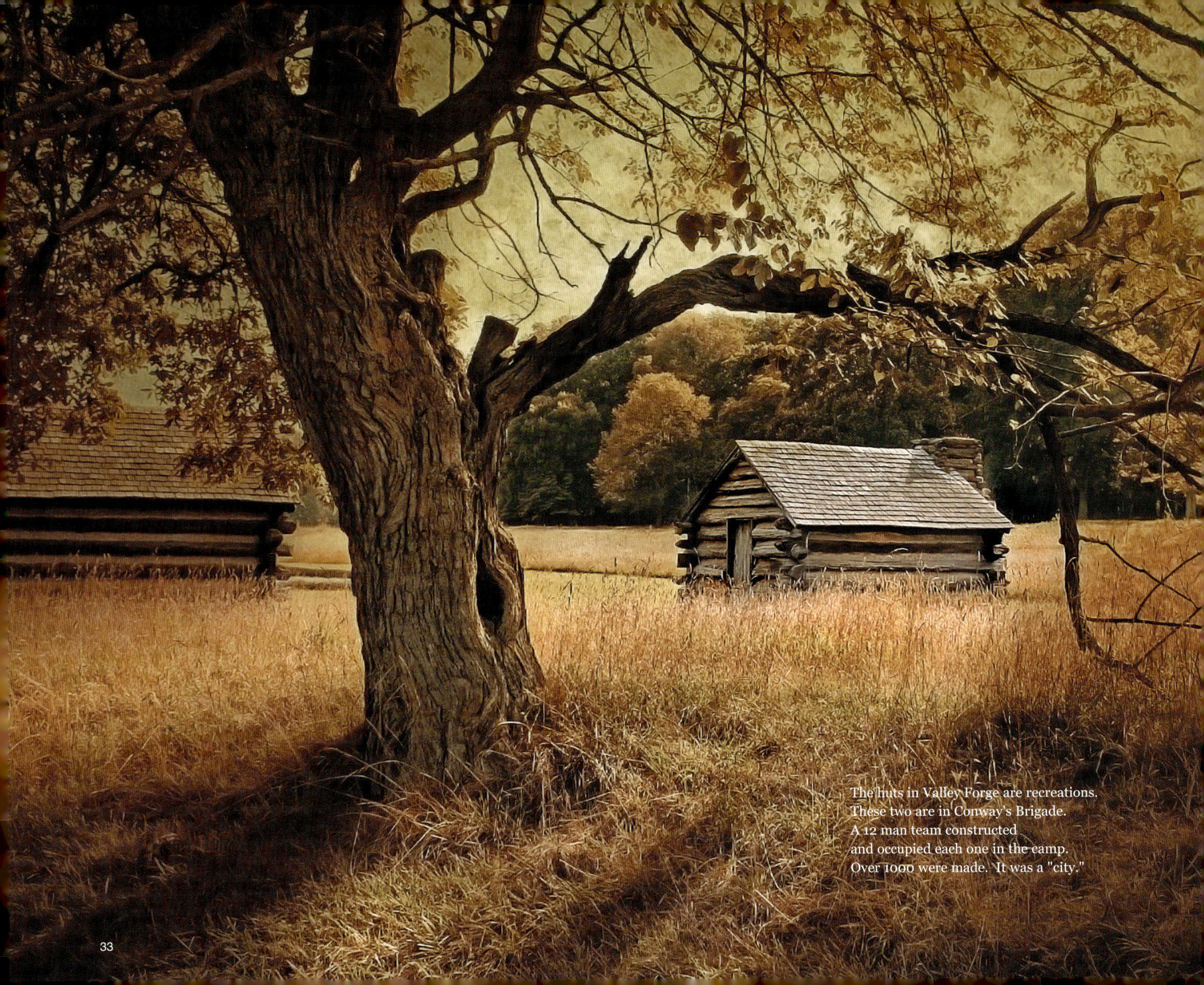

The huts in Valley Forge are recreations.
These two are in Conway's Brigade.
A 12 man team constructed
and occupied each one in the camp.
Over 1000 were made. It was a "city."

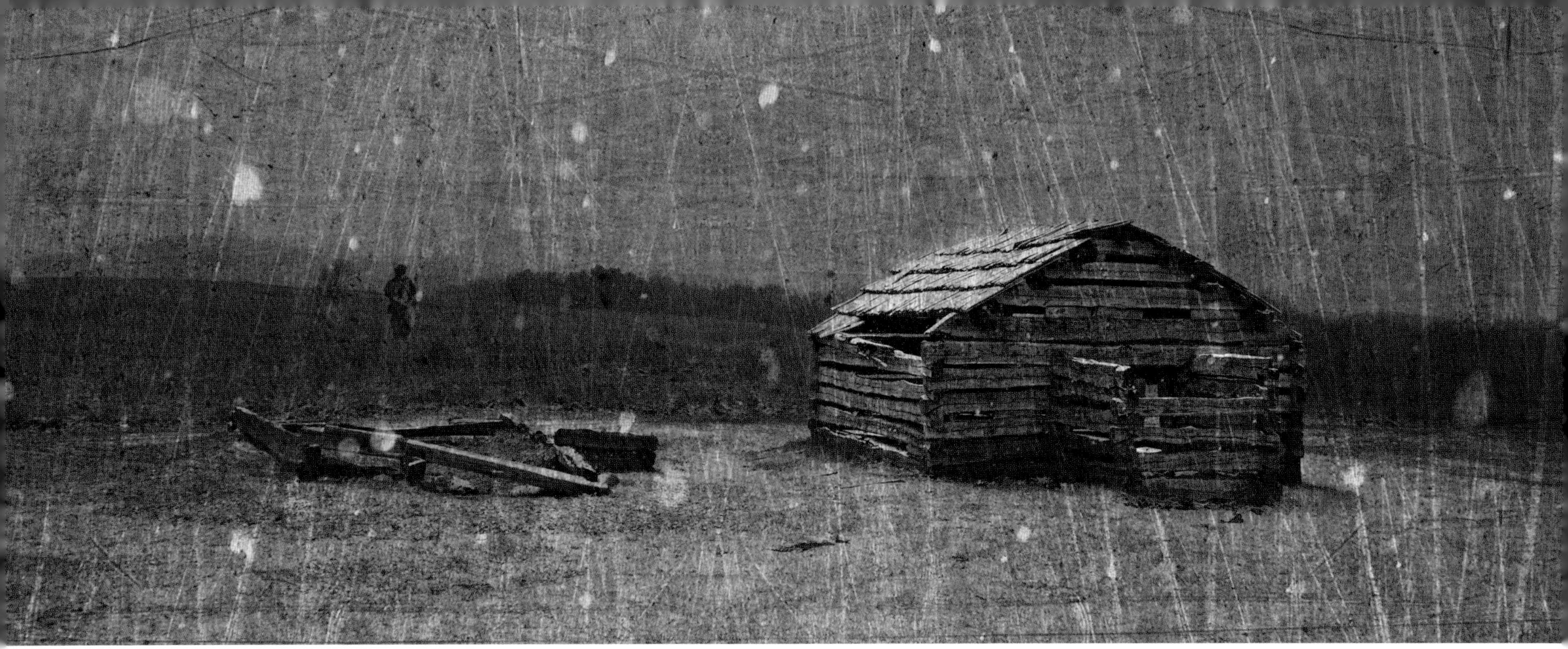

HISTORY LESSON 7: SOLDIERS' QUARTERS

Within days of their arrival at Valley Forge, Continental Army soldiers began building their huts as directed by General Washington. Between December 21 and January 20, hut construction was a top priority. Over 1000 huts were built based on Washington's specific plan for construction, but many men used their own initiative to construct the log huts.

Building one's own log house sounds like great fun until you consider the conditions under which the soldiers were working. The lack of food and proper clothing made it difficult for the men to work outside and to carefully follow orders for hut construction. There were very few tools or animals around to help haul logs. To add to the problems, building materials were scarce. As a result, there was a wide variety in the size, shape, and look of the huts.

There is evidence that some huts were dug into the earth with their floors several feet below ground level. Others were built with fireplaces in the corner. There may have been regional variations in building techniques. Soldiers from North Carolina, for example, may have built their huts differently from those built by soldiers from Pennsylvania.

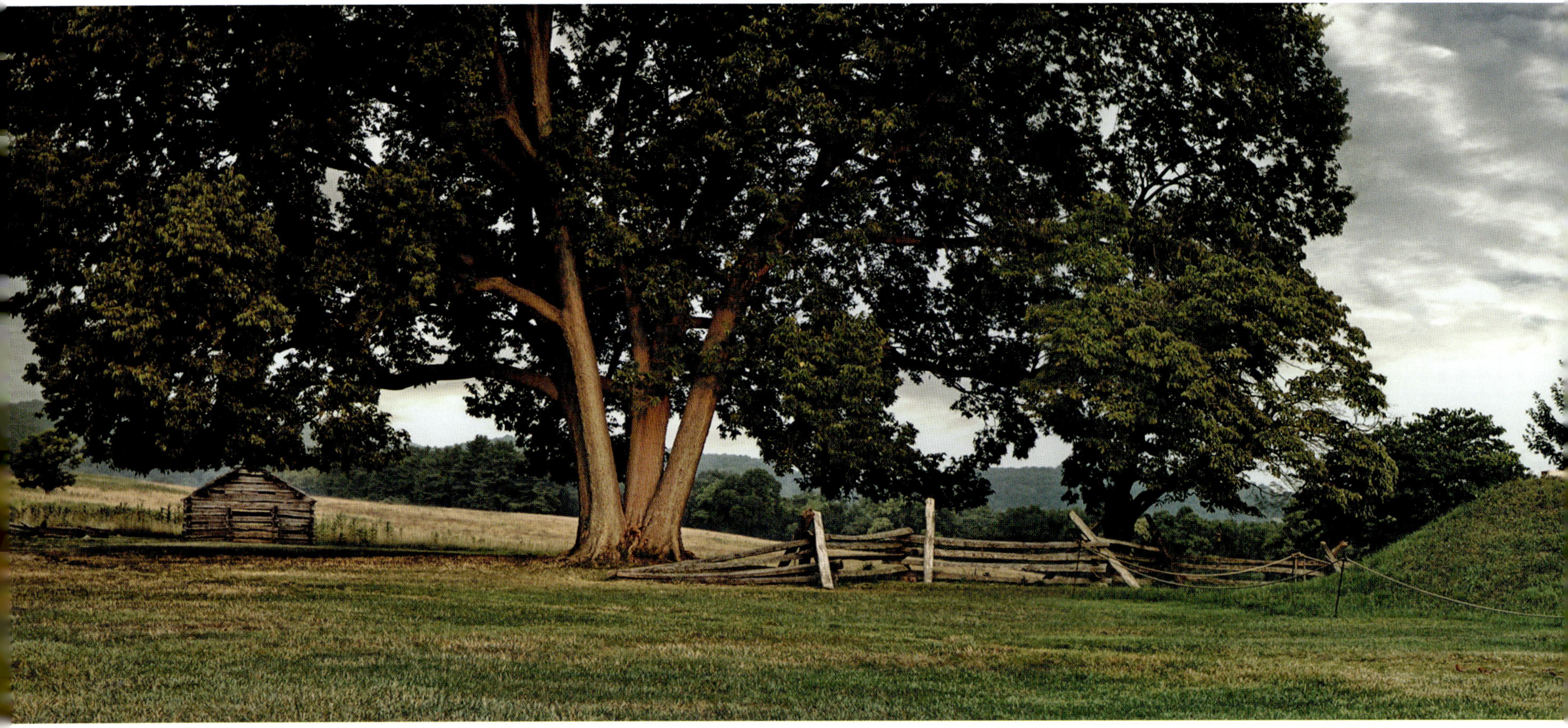

These are two huts in Muhlenberg Brigade and the mound in the middle is a working oven that is used frequently in re-enactments for park guests.

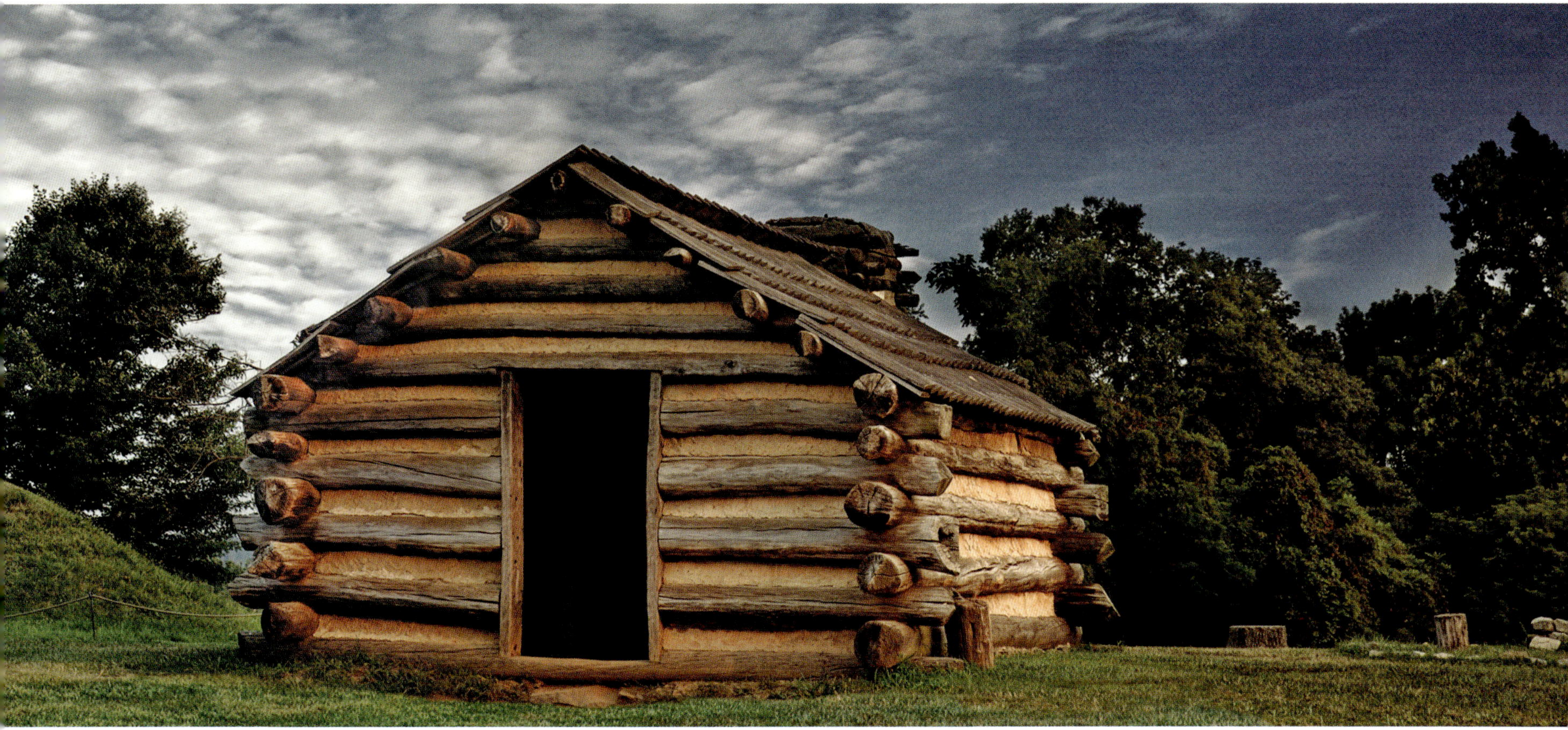

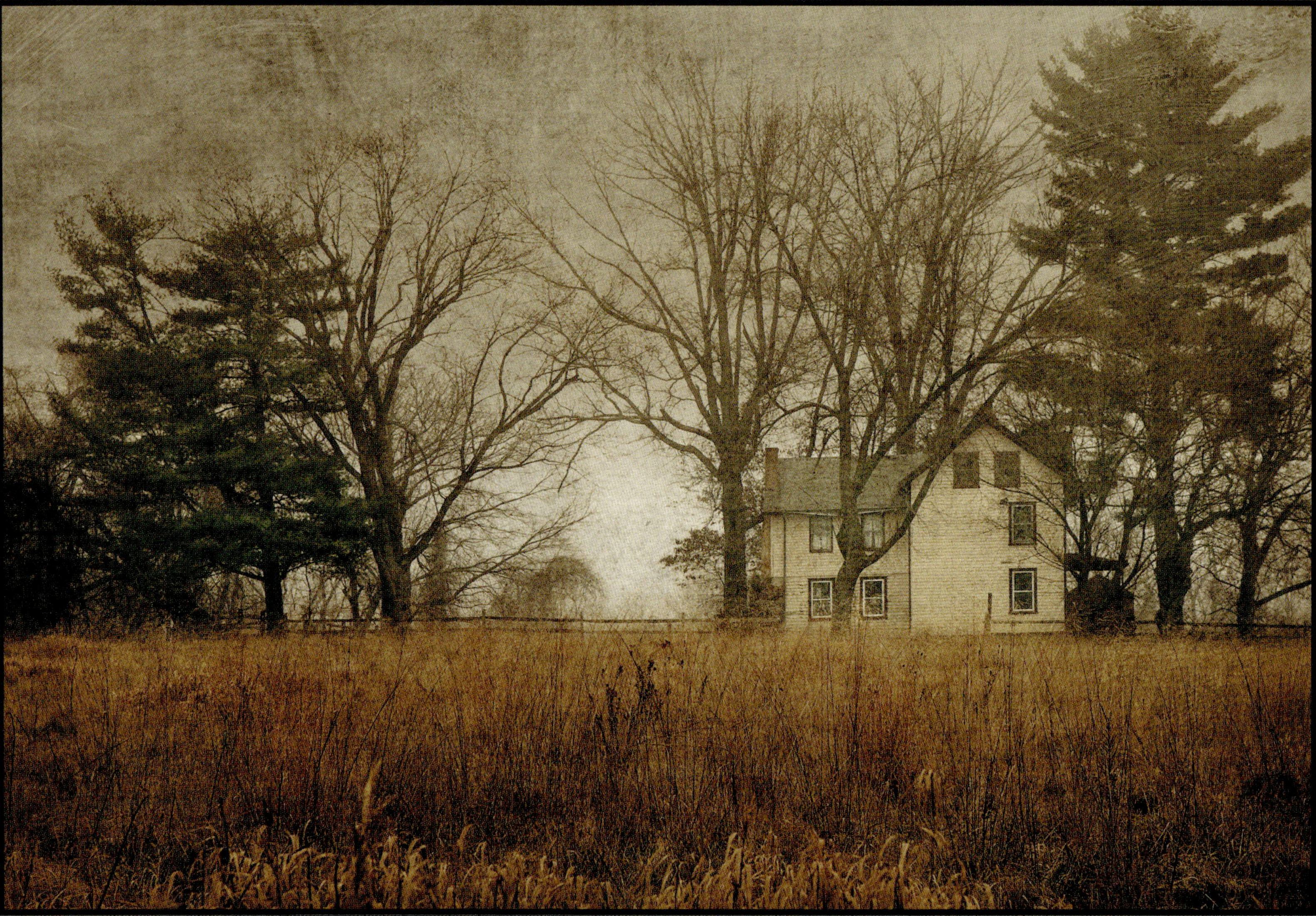

This page and the next are scenes from the North side of the park.
It is an area less traveled by out-of-town guests, but locals know it well.
This is the house at Pawling Farm. The character and charm

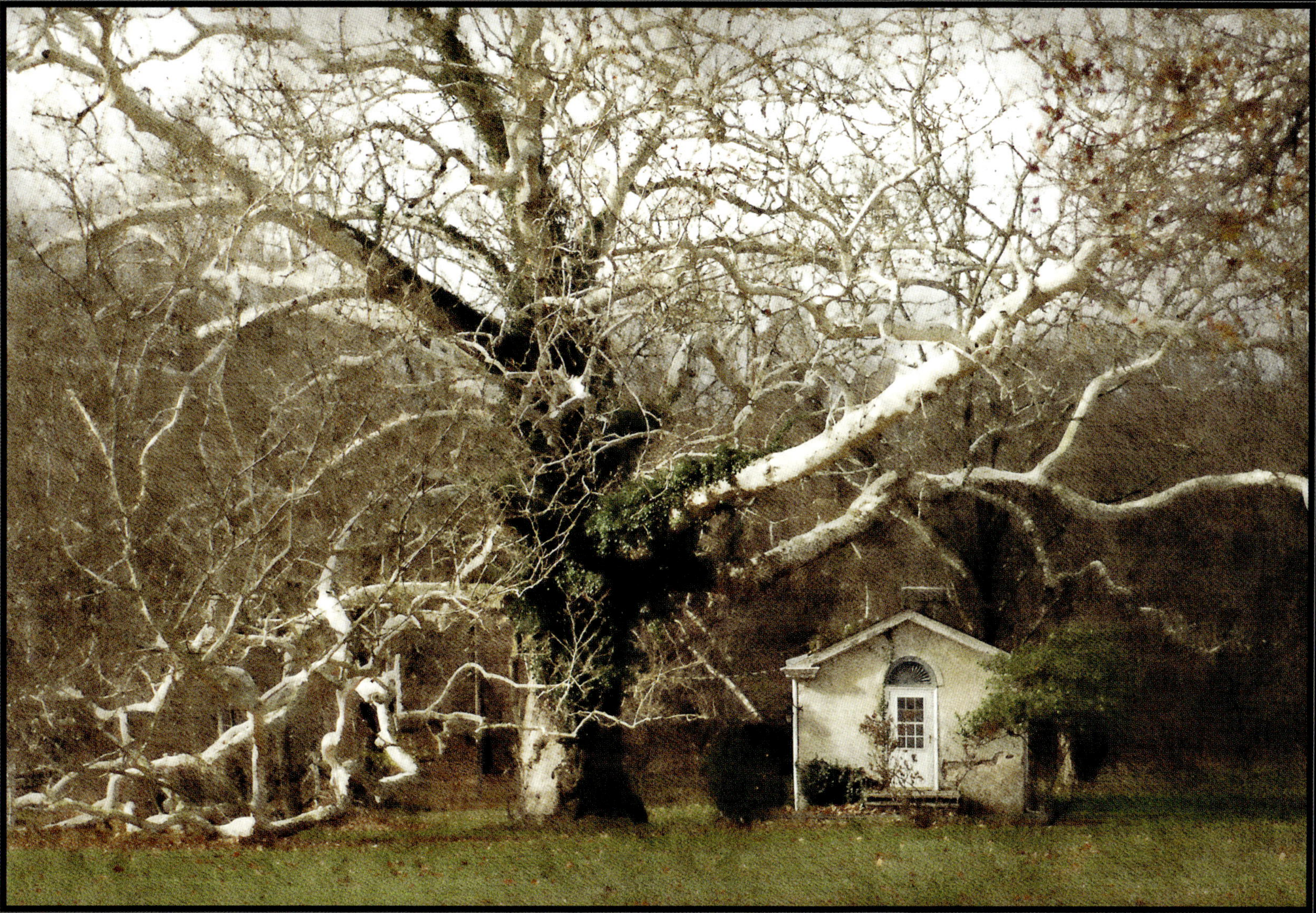

A magnificent sycamore tree lives on the North side near Pawling Farm. This image does little to convey its majesty, you really need to go there and walk around the massive trunk. Although a core sample was never taken for fear of infection it is thought to date back to the mid-1700s.

Beautiful all year but especially in the Fall and Winter when its white bark is most visible.

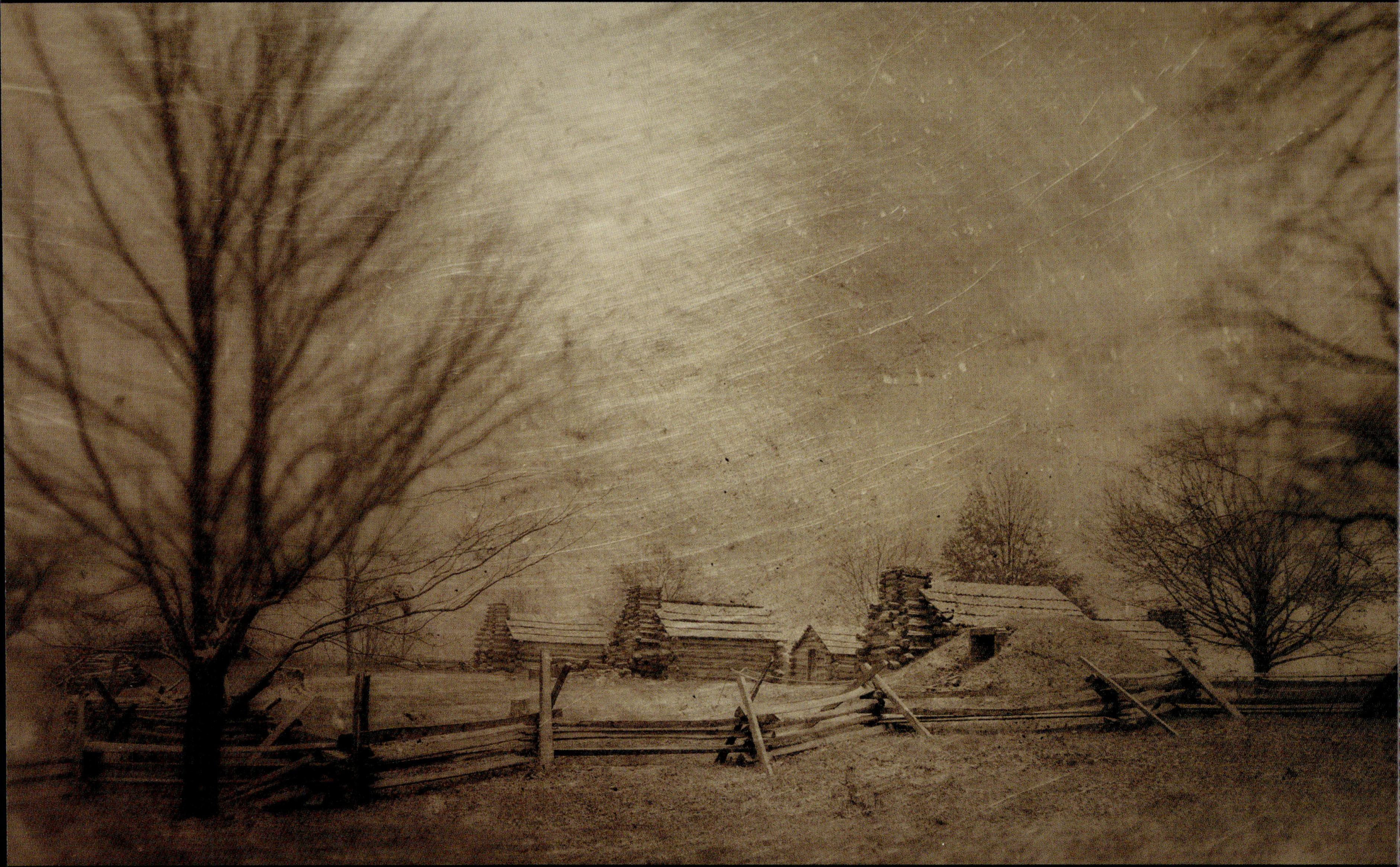

This is my interpretation of how a harsh winter's evening could have looked in 1778 at Muhlenberg's Brigade.

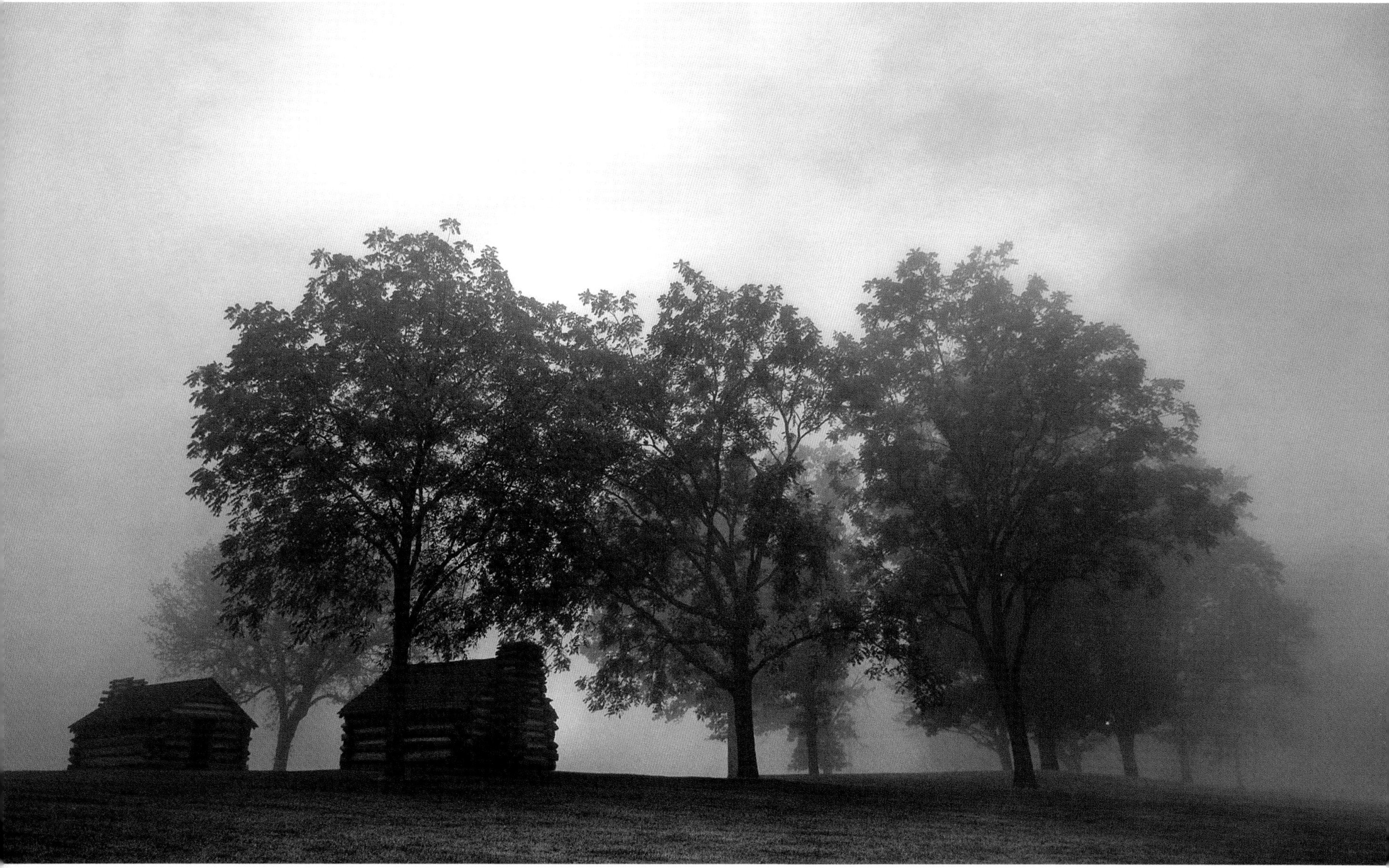

These are two soldier huts along a ridge that runs between the National Memorial Arch and Wayne's Woods. It is another of my favorite shooting areas because of its angle of view. The cover of this book was shot in the same location, just to the left of this scene.

Valley Forge is a place of many moods and a source of personal renewal. I feel very fortunate to live near by and experience those moods in person. It is my hope that you can do the same through these images.

Page(s)	Title
4	*"252 Path"*
5-6	*"Light On The Redoubt"*
7	*"Split Tree"*
8	*"Autumn Leaves"*
9-10	*"Guarding Wayne's Woods"*
11	*"Defiance"*
12	*"Wind Gust"*
13	*"Dripline"*
14	*"Daybreak Encampment"*
15	*"Bluster"*
16	*"Stable In Winter"*
17-18	*"Winter Headquarters"*
19-20	*"Conway's Panorama"*
21	*"Grand Parade Pair"*
22	*"Lean" (lg.)* *"Grand Parade Sycamore" (sm.)*
23	*"Morning Doe"*
24	*"Morning Forage"*
25	*"Redoubt" (sm.)* *"Silence Is Golden" (lg.)*
26	*"Peace In The Valley"*
27-28	*"The Haves And The Have Nots"*
29-30	*"Covered Bridge - 10'0" " (sm.)* *"The Lone Grazer" (lg.)*
31	*"Knox Barn: Colonial Sunset"*
32	*"Across The Knox Bridge"*
33	*"Knot Hole"*
34	*"The Long Walk Home"*
35-36	*"Muhlenberg's Panorama"*
37	*"Gray Morning, North Side"*
38	*"Sycamore"*
39	*"Winter Camp"*
40	*"A Soft Morning In Valley Forge"*

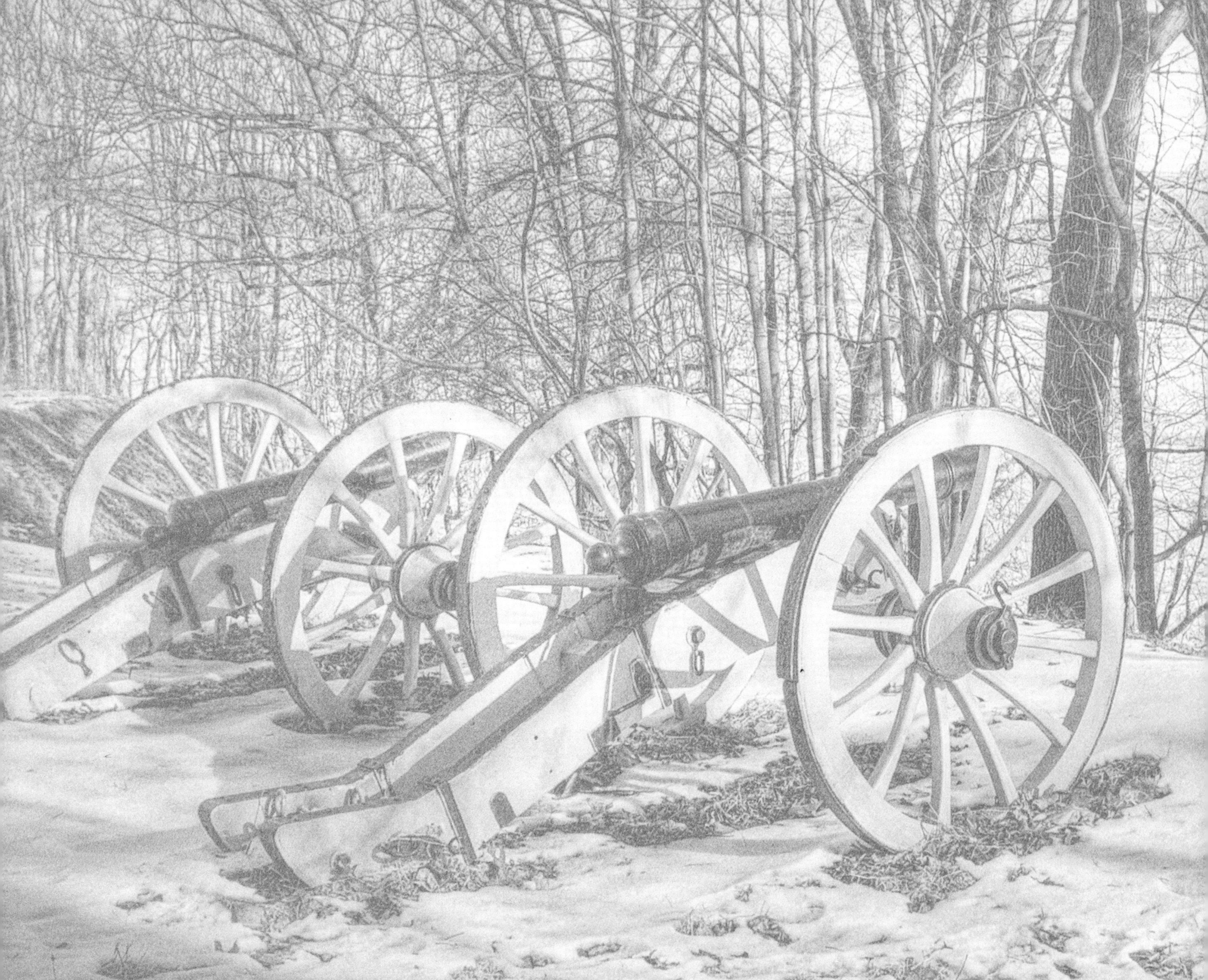